D1180655

THE ULTIMATE DOLLS' HOUSE BOOK

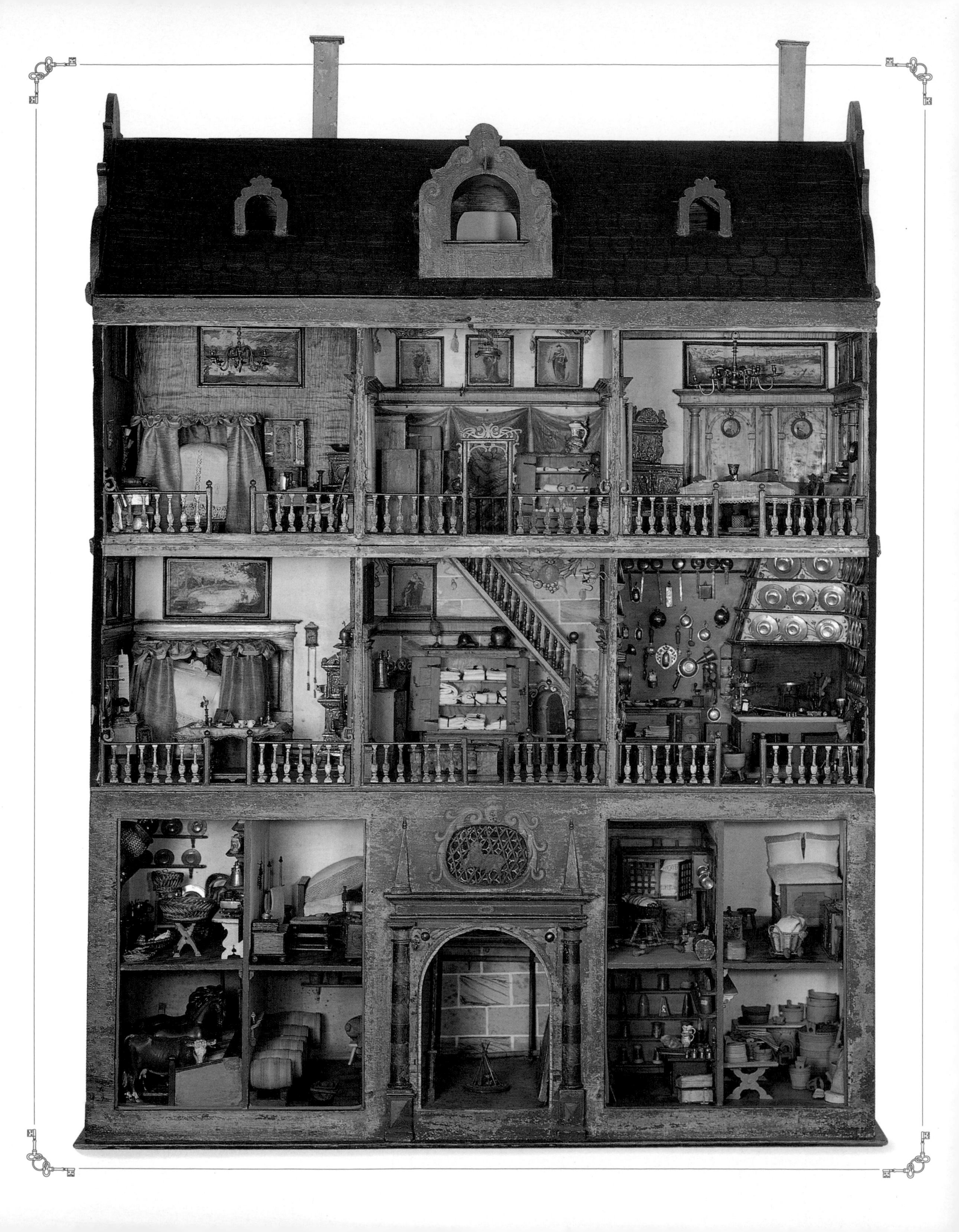

THE ULTIMATE DOLLS' HOUSE BOOK

Faith Eaton

Foreword by
Flora Gill Jacobs

Photography by
Matthew Ward

DORLING KINDERSLEY
London • New York • Stuttgart

A DORLING KINDERSLEY BOOK

Project Editor Irene Lyford
Art Editor Kevin Ryan
Editor Lucinda Hawksley
Computer page make-up Mark Bracey
Production Eunice Paterson, Meryl Silbert
Managing Editor Mary-Clare Jerram
Managing Art Editors Spencer Holbrook, Amanda Lunn

First published in Great Britain in 1994
by Dorling Kindersley Limited,
9 Henrietta Street, London WC2E 8PS

A CIP catalogue record for this book is available from
the British Library

ISBN 0 7513 0112 4

Text film output by The Right Type, Great Britain
Reproduction by Colourscan, Singapore
Printed and bound in Italy by New Interlitho

Contents

FOREWORD

Flora Gill Jacobs

IN A DOLLS' HOUSE, "time stands still and a period is preserved as it never can be in a full-sized house. All sorts of things, however ephemeral, are left in a dolls' house that would never remain in a human's".

PLAYTIME *(ABOVE) To countless small girls in the past, their dolls' houses were well-loved playthings that gave no hint of the role they were to assume, generations later, as reflections of domestic history.*

These are words of mine in the 1965 edition of *A History of Dolls' Houses*. They are repeated here, not only because they help to explain the role of an antique dolls' house as a historical document, but because they relate to a coincidence. "There can be no better example," I continued, "than a nearly modern dolls' house played with in the grim, dark London days of World War II by Miss Faith Eaton, a gifted English doll-maker and collector." The author of this beautiful book had once written to me to describe her 1940 dolls' house with its "air raid shelter ... brown sticky paper crosses on its windows, and black-out curtains". Faith Eaton crossed the pages of my book and now, briefly, I cross the pages of hers. I have always maintained that the dolls' house world is small in all respects, and here is yet another example.

MEXICAN HOUSE *(BELOW) Found in 1977, covered with dust, in an antique shop in Puebla, Mexico, this mansion is now referred to by the Washington Dolls' House & Toy Museum as its extravaganza. The house, which is 228cm (90in) high and 183cm (72in) wide, features a chapel, an aviary, a working lift, and a roof garden.*

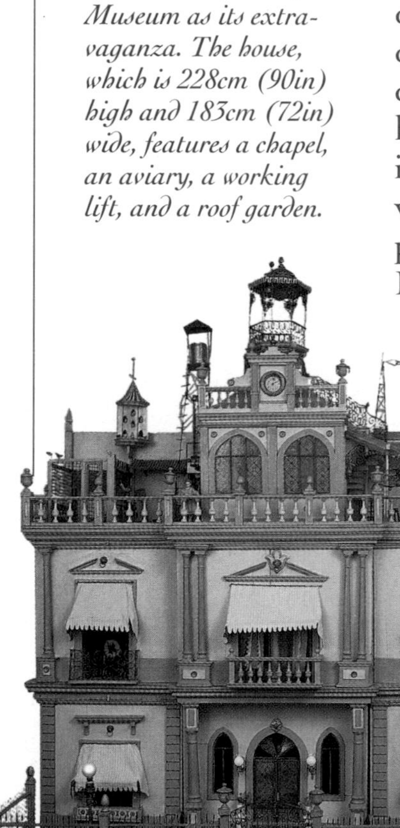

Small it may be, but this miniature world has expanded greatly in recent years. There has been a renaissance, in which collectors have been collecting old dolls' houses, furnishing new ones, organizing "miniature" clubs, and arranging fairs where dolls' houses and their contents are sold. Books about dolls' houses also have proliferated.

— BIRTH OF A COLLECTOR —

When, in 1945, I embarked upon a history of dolls' houses, and then started to collect (a reversal of the usual procedure), there had never been a "history". At the turn of the century, a learned volume was published in German and Dutch about the magnificent seventeenth- and eighteenth-century Dutch *puppenhuizen*, and there had been books about the elaborate dolls' house presented to Queen Mary by her subjects in 1924. But most antique-dealers were slow to notice the charming possibilities that remained in attics till decades later. When I visited London in 1948, several weeks spent prowling in antique shops for old dolls' houses and their furnishings produced only a couple of chairs and a settee.

UPPARK *(ABOVE)*
The nine rooms in this English baby house (each opening separately) are all beautifully furnished, and are occupied by correctly costumed dolls. The house was taken to Uppark in Sussex in 1747 by Miss Sarah Lethieullier when she married Sir Matthew Fetherstonhaugh.

— GROWING TREND —

In 1975, when the Washington Dolls' House & Toy Museum opened to the public, there were collections or isolated examples in public museums in Britain, Europe, and the United States, and there was Vivien Greene's private museum in Oxford. Small doll museums, with antique dolls on shelves and an odd house nearby, were not unusual. In recent years, however, dolls' house museums have been opening on both sides of the Atlantic. Dolls' houses have become, with many collectors, not only a preoccupation but an addiction – one that is often associated with a degree of dissatisfaction with today's world.

But there is another lure to the dolls' house, which has always existed – an element that was described by A.C. Benson (co-editor with Sir Lawrence Weaver of *The Book of the Queen's Dolls' House*) in words that have never yet been surpassed: "There is great beauty in smallness. One gets all the charm of design and colour and effect, because you can see so much more in combination and juxaposition ...."

In other words, dolls' houses are not only historic, documenting in miniature the architecture, decorative arts, and daily life that they reflect, but they are also seductive. With this volume, illustrated by Matthew Ward's exquisite pictures, which are almost *trompe l'oeil* in their effect, another wave of dolls' house collectors is almost certain to be seduced.

CHRISTIAN HACKER HOUSE *(BELOW)*
This house, made in Nuremberg c.1900, is typical of those created by Christian Hacker. Although some aspects of designs varied to some extent, other features, such as the lift-off mansard roof and the "French" look illustrated here, were invariably maintained.

INTRODUCTION

Miniatures have an irresistible fascination for both adults and children: adults are intrigued by the skill and artistry involved in the creation of tiny objects, while children are simply entranced. When the doors of a complete miniature house are opened, revealing comfortably furnished bedrooms, an elegant drawing-room, or a kitchen equipped with every utensil imaginable, the magic is complete. We hope that within these pages you too will experience the enchantment.

THERE IS NO AGE LIMIT for dolls' house enthusiasts. For many their involvement has grown up with them, having first focused on a childhood plaything; some develop their interest by way of related subjects, such as architecture, interior design, or social history; yet others may discover, in their second childhood, a pleasure that they were denied in their first. The fascination of miniature replicas has been experienced since the days of ancient Greece and Rome but, for many dolls' house collectors, the most interesting part of the long history of miniature houses and their furnishings began in the countries of northern Europe, around the middle of the seventeenth century.

DUTCH CABINET *(LEFT)*
Petronella de la Court's late-seventeenth-century cabinet house reflects the splendour and elegance that epitomized such affluent Dutch collectors' homes. The cabinet itself is a magnificent piece of furniture, and most of the miniature pieces it contains are beautiful objets d'art.

— NATIONAL VARIATIONS —

Most dolls' house collectors in the seventeenth and eighteenth centuries lived in Germany, Holland, or in England. The interiors of their miniature houses reflected their own lifestyles, illustrating how their homes were furnished. The type of casing chosen to house the collections differed from country to country, however.

German women believed that it was important to teach their young daughters how to be good housewives, so they tended to use miniature houses as educational toys. This is not to say that the children were allowed to treat these small replicas as playthings –

TOO OLD TO PLAY *(ABOVE)*
The two-roomed dolls' house shown in this detail from an oil-painting by Harry Brooker (1848–1941) was obviously a well-loved plaything, which was enjoyed by both boys and girls.

HAMLEYS HOUSE *(RIGHT)*
This house (see pp.96–97) *was a "modern" design when it came from Hamleys toy-shop as a birthday present in the early 1930s. It is now in honourable retirement in my collection.*

only the room settings that were furnished as kitchens served in this dual capacity – but at least the children were permitted some involvement with what were essentially adults' treasures.

German miniature houses were often elaborately furnished, and were equipped with every household necessity. Although most of them had realistic roofs and side walls, the models usually lacked fronts: the importance of these miniature houses lay with their contents and furnishings, so a facade would have served no particular purpose.

Affluent Dutch men and women were often keen collectors of porcelain, paintings, and fine furniture, as well as miniature replicas. As the latter were often very valuable, they were sometimes housed inside a fine cabinet or cupboard that had been designed and adapted to look like the interior of a house.

Dutch cabinet houses, like the German dolls' houses, lacked a realistic, house-like facade; the cabinet doors hid and protected the miniature contents within, and served to emphasize the value of the collectors' possessions. Sara Ploos van Amstel and Petronella de la Court were both particularly enthusiastic Dutch collectors; two of their exquisite cabinet houses are featured in this book *(see pp.24–29; 34–37)*.

English collectors in the seventeenth and eighteenth centuries had quite a different attitude. For

WAX DOLLS *(LEFT)*
The well-preserved wax dolls in Petronella de la Court's cabinet house (see pp.24–29) *are all correctly and beautifully dressed in late-seventeenth-century costumes.*

MANWARING HOUSE
(ABOVE) According to family tradition, this baby house (displayed in Farnham Museum, Hampshire) was made by John Manwaring, c.1788, for his four daughters. The interior is unfurnished, but the house has a double staircase and a German-style parapet across both upper storeys.

NUREMBERG KITCHEN
(BELOW) The Nuremberg kitchen, filled with tiny implements and utensils, was an excellent teaching toy. This fine seventeenth-century example (see pp.56–57) *is exhibited in the Washington Dolls' House & Toy Museum, Washington, D.C., USA.*

them a baby house was exactly what the description suggested: a small replica of a house with a realistic facade – one that may have been loosely based on, or even deliberately designed to replicate, their own home.

A large number of early dolls' houses and room sets still exist. These are displayed in museums, both national and privately owned, in Europe and North America, and offer a fascinating insight into life-styles and fashions over the centuries.

— CONTEMPORARY CRAFTSMEN —

Though dolls' house collections nowadays tend to be a combination of adults' and children's "toys", modern examples are usually furnished with at least some pieces made by craftsmen, rather than entirely with mass-produced items. Stimulated by the immense revival of interest in small replica miniatures that has been expressed by collectors, a number of twentieth-century miniaturists are now creating models of such fine quality that they equal any that were made in past centuries.

It would appear that the wheel has spun full circle, back to the days when collectors were commissioning craftsmen to make fine miniatures for their cabinets and baby houses. There is one intriguing difference, however. Two hundred years ago, collectors were not merely collecting and displaying miniature

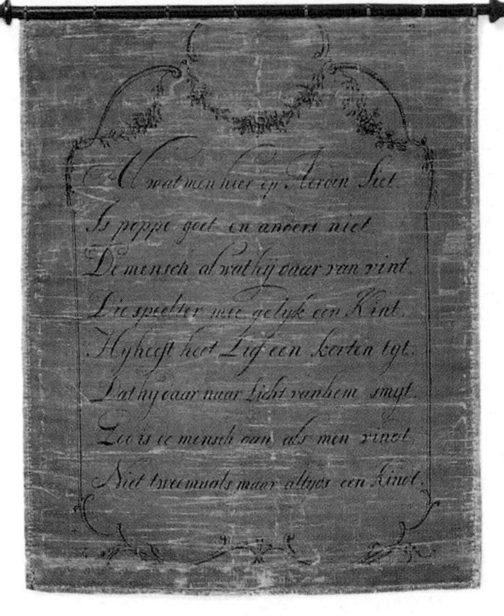

WALL HANGING *(LEFT)* *A scroll, with a hand-written verse* (see below), *hangs in the lying-in room of Sara Ploos van Amstel's cabinet house* (see pp.34–37).

MODERN ROOM SET *(RIGHT) This room set, fitted with modern American-style furniture, is from a section in my collection that records contemporary ways of life. The occupants work at home, using the latest technology.*

replicas; they were also deliberately recording their own life-styles and homes. This is illustrated by Sara Ploos van Amstel's insistence that the unusual basement dining-room in her Amsterdam home should be replicated in one of her cabinet houses; it is also inherent in her philosophy, which is expressed in the words on the tiny scroll hanging in the lying-in room in that cabinet house:

> *Everything one sees on earth*
> *Is dolls' stuff, and nothing else.*
> *All that man finds*
> *He plays with like a child.*
> *Ardently he loves for a short while*
> *What he throws away so easily thereafter.*
> *Thus man is, as one finds,*
> *Not only once but always a child.*

Only a few twentieth-century collectors seem to share their ancestors' desire to record their life-styles in miniature; for most, revelling in the past seems preferable to illustrating the present. In the United Kingdom, for example, classic Georgian-style mansions and ornate Victorian town-houses are almost always preferred to dolls' houses that depict today's architecture.

— MINIATURE MASTERPIECES —

There is, however, one magnificent example of a twentieth-century miniature house that was designed to display the skills of contemporary British artists and craftsmen, and to provide a record of the life-style of the British monarchy in the twentieth century. The house was designed by Sir Edwin Lutyens and presented to Queen Mary, wife of Britain's King George V, in 1924. Although miniature *objets d'art*, with or without rooms or houses, have long been regarded as suitable gifts for royalty, this is one of the finest ever made; and it was an inspired offering, as the Queen was passionately interested in furniture, interior decoration, and in collecting miniatures.

Today the house stands behind its glass screens in Windsor Castle, unaltered and immaculate even after 70 years *(see p.16)*. But, although it is still called Queen Mary's Dolls' House, the one thing this magnificent miniature building is not, and never should be called, is a dolls' house. Sometimes the distinction between a dolls' house and a miniature house is arguable, but not in this instance; this house is a perfect example of the miniaturist's art, and no doll has ever set foot in it.

MODERN MINIATURES *(BELOW)* *Pieces such as this Chippendale-style chair and the circular rent table, both made by John Hodgson for the Georgian House* (see pp.48–51), *illustrate the fine work of today's miniaturists.*

GRECON DOLLS *(LEFT)* *"Grecon" was the trade name for the wool- and wire-bodied dolls, with cloth heads and metal feet, created by Grete Cohn in the 1940s and 1950s.*

When a miniature house or set of rooms has been created in order to display examples of the miniaturist's art, or to illustrate the furniture and decor of a certain period, or to reproduce a particular historic house, the illusion of reality can be marred, and the viewer distracted, by the presence of even the most life-like doll.

Two dedicated collectors who were both determined to record, in meticulous detail, period styles of architecture and furnishings in their sets of rooms – Mrs Carlisle in England and Mrs Thorne in the United States – both chose to leave their rooms unoccupied. It is interesting that the women were assembling their rooms, quite independently, from the 1920s to the 1950s, and never met or corresponded.

The sumptuously furnished and decorated rooms of the early Dutch, German, and English cabinets and baby houses, on the other hand, were usually inhabited by elaborately and authentically costumed dolls. These delicate wax figures generally enhanced their surroundings by adding a "human" dimension.

John Hodgson, a leading British miniaturist, chose modelled figurines, with meticulously painted features, for his miniature buildings at Hever Castle *(see pp.48–51)* as he believes these convey a greater impression of movement and realism than conventional dolls' house dolls.

— VALUABLE SURVIVORS —

Of course "proper" (that is, children's) dolls' houses do need occupants, and collectors today pay huge amounts for miniature dolls' house dolls that their original owners purchased with pocket-money. Little pegged wooden dolls (of which children could buy four for a penny in the 1890s), may now sell for £150 each (dressed) or £60–£80 (undressed) at auction today. It is amazing that so many of these fragile little playthings have survived; even if they have lost the odd limb or feature, and probably all their clothes, they still retain their ability to charm.

And so do their houses. Whether battered playthings or immaculate models, such is their appeal that most people instantly relate to them; perhaps not always with the delight collectors would deem appropriate, but few, surely, can remain unmoved by the sight of a teapot not much bigger than a tea-leaf, or a Georgian mansion balanced on a card-table.

JAPANESE MODEL *(ABOVE) Models such as this were designed as ornaments, for display purposes only. It is not a true dolls' house, but a replica of a traditional-style Japanese house.*

JAPANESE CLASS *(RIGHT) These Japanese doll pupils and their teacher, complete with their original bamboo chairs and tiny blackboard, were exported in the 1890s. (They never had a class-room.)*

NOSTELL PRIORY BABY HOUSE

The Nostell Priory baby house is one of the most magnificent and well-preserved examples of its kind. The fact that it is still housed in the stately home in Yorkshire, England, where it was first created, makes it all the more intriguing.

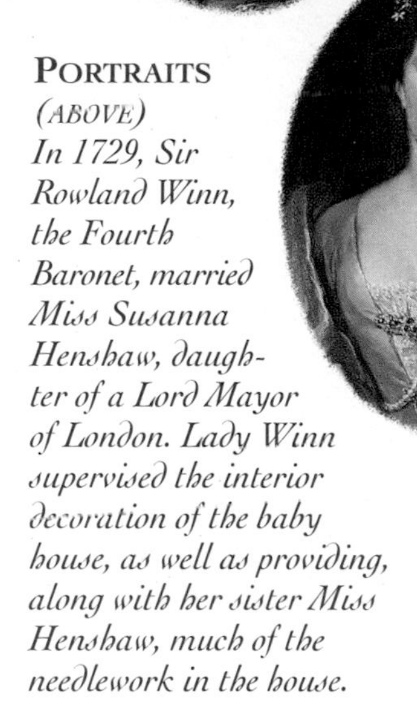

PORTRAITS *(ABOVE)*
In 1729, Sir Rowland Winn, the Fourth Baronet, married Miss Susanna Henshaw, daughter of a Lord Mayor of London. Lady Winn supervised the interior decoration of the baby house, as well as providing, along with her sister Miss Henshaw, much of the needlework in the house.

MANY CONJECTURES have been made about the origins of Nostell's famed baby house, including the belief that Thomas Chippendale was involved in its construction, but no concrete evidence exists on this point. It is known that it was begun in 1735, around the same time as work started on Sir Rowland Winn's new house in the grounds of Nostell Priory. The baby house was predominantly an adult "toy", filled with *objets d'art* and reflecting the life-style of its owner, Lady Winn. Although the baby house shares a number of similarities with Nostell Priory, which was redesigned many times and includes modifications by James Paine and Robert Adam, it also bears a resemblance to the Winn's previous home, at Thornton Curtis, Lincolnshire (particularly its staircase). Interestingly the baby house features a balustrade and statues on the roof, ideas that Robert Adam suggested *c.*1780 for Nostell, but which were never put into effect.

THE FACADE
The fine proportions of the Nostell Priory baby house are best appreciated when you can see the whole facade, from the balustraded roof to the false basement section.

SERVANT DOLLS *(ABOVE)*
The dolls of the house are meticulously dressed in mid-eighteenth-century style.

STATELY HOME *(LEFT)*
A print of Nostell Priory from the time when it was the seat of Charles Winn (1795–1874).

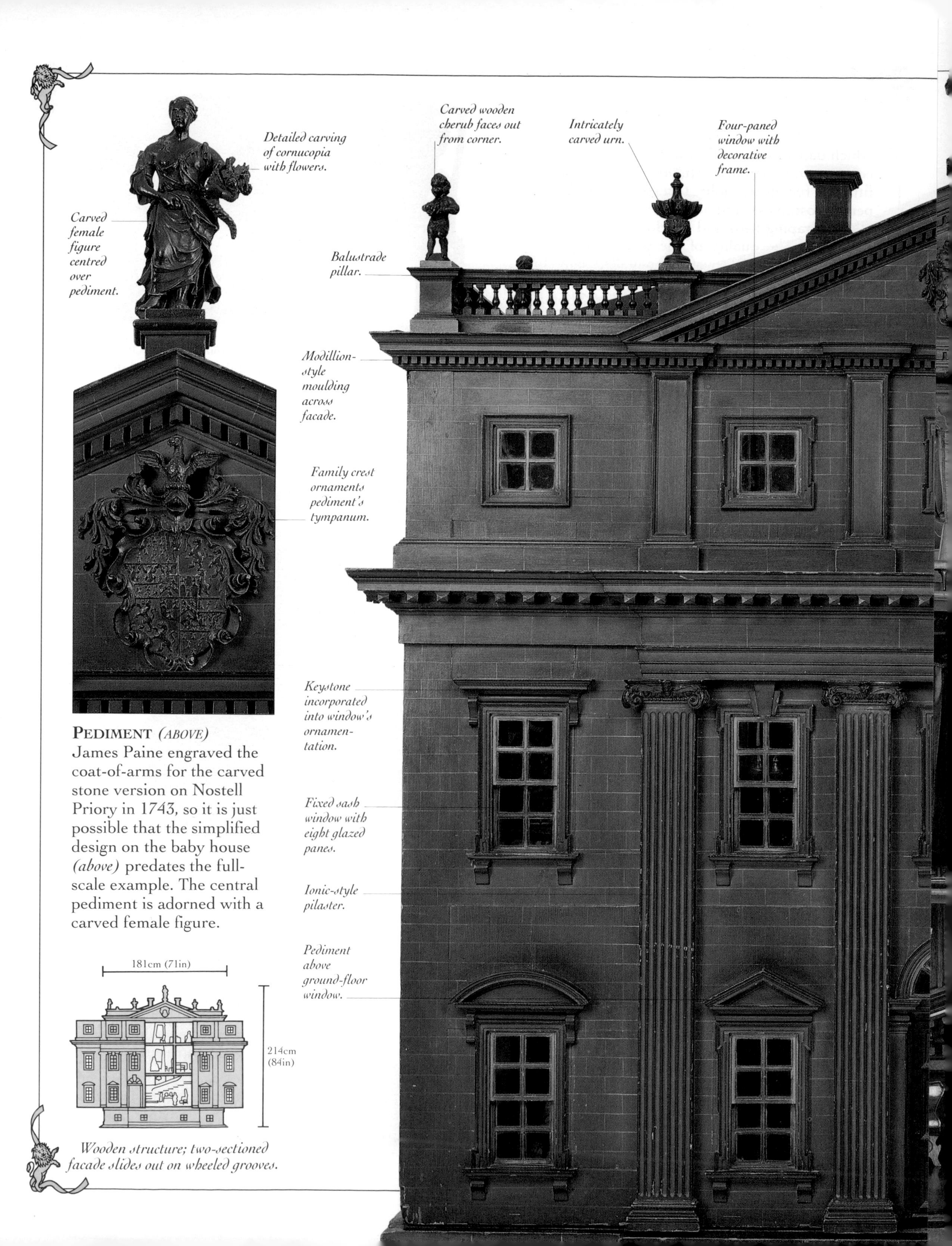

PEDIMENT *(ABOVE)*
James Paine engraved the coat-of-arms for the carved stone version on Nostell Priory in 1743, so it is just possible that the simplified design on the baby house *(above)* predates the full-scale example. The central pediment is adorned with a carved female figure.

Wooden structure; two-sectioned facade slides out on wheeled grooves.

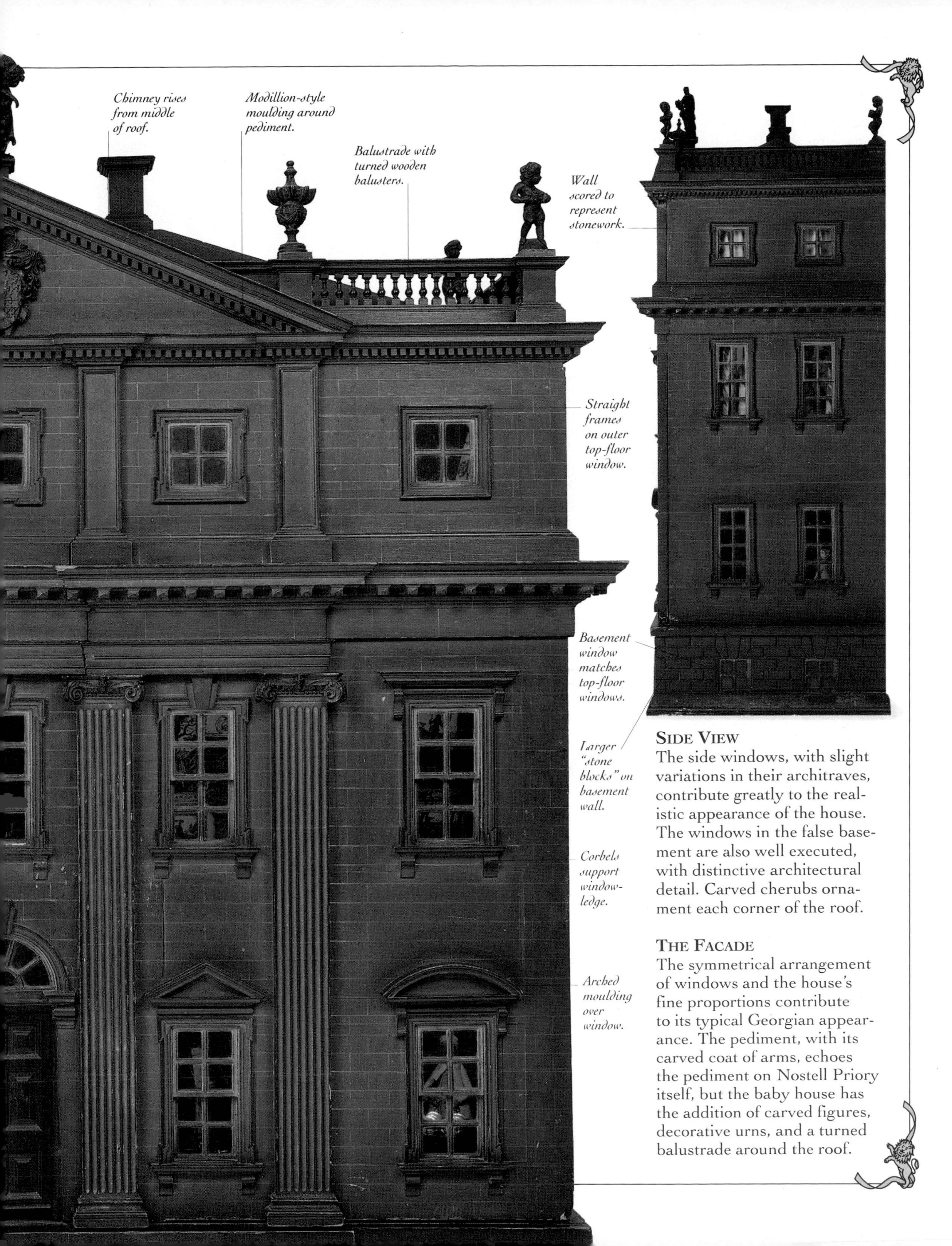

SIDE VIEW

The side windows, with slight variations in their architraves, contribute greatly to the realistic appearance of the house. The windows in the false basement are also well executed, with distinctive architectural detail. Carved cherubs ornament each corner of the roof.

THE FACADE

The symmetrical arrangement of windows and the house's fine proportions contribute to its typical Georgian appearance. The pediment, with its carved coat of arms, echoes the pediment on Nostell Priory itself, but the baby house has the addition of carved figures, decorative urns, and a turned balustrade around the roof.

Mid-eighteenth-century English Dolls

THE NOSTELL PRIORY BABY HOUSE seems caught in a time-warp, and its dolls, wearing well-preserved mid-eighteenth-century costumes, make fitting occupants for such a mansion. Much may be learned about the fashions of that period from the dolls' dress: the women and the little girls wear authentic, detailed replicas of the outer garments that were popular at that time, over correctly styled petticoats and shoes. The cream dress with a red pattern is particularly interesting, as the design is finely embroidered in the correct scale for its wearer. Sadly, the only male dolls of the household now remaining are the footman and the cook.

THE LADIES *(BELOW)*
All of the dolls have well-modelled wax heads and hands, and realistic hair-styles. They have been beautifully dressed, with meticulous attention to detail (probably by Lady Winn and her sister). The most elegantly attired (and tallest) doll wears a red silk overdress, over a white silk underskirt, and high-heeled wax boots.

MALE SERVANTS *(RIGHT)*
Nostell's servant dolls are made of painted wood, in the English tradition. The footman wears Winn livery and the cook is dressed in immaculate linen.

The Collection

In this unique collection of miniature houses we offer a broad view of the dolls' house world. Not just adult treasures from the seventeenth and eighteenth centuries, and exquisite nineteenth-century models: our selection also includes twentieth-century children's toys and specially commissioned models from museums and private collections around the world.

• Hobbies House •

Now a collectors' item, this typical late-1920s English dolls' house was made from plans printed by Hobbies of Dereham.

STROMER HOUSE

South German; dated 1639

THIS FASCINATING HOUSE, which provides an amazing record of the rooms in an affluent seventeenth-century German home, was presented to the Germanisches National Museum in 1879 by Baron von Stromer – hence the house's popular name (the original owner is unknown).

The rooms are cleverly rather than realistically positioned within an open-fronted structure with a central doorway; the sides are painted to represent walls with bottle-glass windows. The internal scale varies, the rooms in the base section being smaller than those in the upper floors – possibly in order to fit in more rooms. Curiously, the casing of the base also differs and, like the roof, was once removable.

Wooden chimney fixed at back of house.

Dormer window with pulley above.

Ornamental gable-end.

Figure of lion set into oval lattice window.

THE FACADE
The house has no facade, but the roof features traditionally shaped gables and windows, including a central dormer on which is painted the date "1639".

ENTRANCE DOORS *(BELOW)*
The two arched doors have a *trompe l'oeil* effect suggesting a vaulted interior.

156cm (61½in)

235cm (92½in)

Open-fronted wooden structure; divided into 15 sections.

Entrance doors show trompe l'oeil *tiled porch floor.*

Papered wood-grain-effect walls.

Well-filled duvet and mattress increase height of bed.

Fine lawn nightshirt laid out on bed.

Barber's bowl hangs from peg.

Panelling extends only to foot of bed, avoiding stove area.

Balustrade across front of room.

Basket of provisions in store-room.

Second Floor
Both the comfortably furnished bedroom *(left)* and the reception-room *(right)* are heated by green ceramic stoves. The ceiling in the hall is painted, as is a decorative frieze. Several fine landscapes and religious paintings hang in the reception-room in the area between the panelled walls and the ceiling.

Canopy over hearth useful for warming pewter plates.

First Floor
The wood-panelled bedroom *(left)* is heated by a ceramic stove, and a well-stocked linen cupboard stands on the richly decorated central landing. In the kitchen *(right)* is an eye-catching display of metalware, including several shelves of pewter plates around the chimney-breast and on both side walls.

Decorated meat-safe beside hearth.

Baby's bassinet on wheels.

Ground Floor
On each side of the entrance hall, with its painted "cobblestone" floor, stone-effect walls, and poultry cage, is a set of four small rooms, representing stables and a wine-cellar *(left)*, with a store-room and servant's bedroom above; and an office/store-room and laundry *(right)*, with two small nurseries above.

Simple but well-equipped laundry.

Germanisches National Museum, Nuremberg

GERMAN AFFLUENCE

THE STROMER HOUSE contains many rare and informative examples of a well-to-do family's possessions in seventeenth-century Germany, as well as spectacular use of wall-painting and *trompe l'oeil*. Such provision makes the lack of occupants regrettable; unused nurseries contain toys and cradles, bedrooms have nightshirts laid out, and no fewer than three linen cupboards store the necessities for the absent household.

CRADLE *(RIGHT)*
A baby could be gently rocked to sleep in this decorative and practical swinging-cradle, which is built onto a matching chest with two drawers. It is constructed of plain wood with applied fret-work decoration.

Lace-trimmed lawn coverlet protects cradle's bedding.

Cradle support incorporated into two-drawer chest.

Drawer holds linen for baby and cradle.

Nutmeg representing ostrich egg in decorative stand.

Metal helmet with visor.

Miniature metal breastplate.

Strong metal hinge on linen cupboard.

Inner surface of door shows back of fretwork panel.

Bundle of clean linen tied with coloured ribbon.

Beaded basket for toilet items.

Metal water cistern.

Small metal bell.

Wooden-handled clothes brush.

Brackets originally held water cistern.

Large sponge attached by cord to hook.

Metal wash-basin on curved wooden stand.

Ornamental brush hanging on hook.

Hinged lower cupboard door.

Metal bed-warmer on stand.

LINEN CUPBOARD *(ABOVE)*
Although German linen cupboards tend to be practical rather than beautiful pieces of furniture, they were often placed in reception rooms or on landings, like this fine natural wood example.

WASH-STAND *(RIGHT)*
A metal water cistern (now stored upside-down on top of the wash-stand) originally hung from brackets above the basin. Two cupboards with panelled doors are built into the wash-stand.

CEILING SECTION *(ABOVE)*
The boldly painted ceiling of the top-floor landing, along with the delicate frieze, fine paintings, and *trompe l'oeil* curtains on the back wall, give the room a sumptuous air.

Strings attached to pegs.
Open top allows mechanism to be seen.
Keyboard with five black and eight "white" keys.

VIRGINAL *(ABOVE)*
This instrument, a table-top version of the harpsichord, was popular in the sixteenth and seventeenth centuries, especially with young ladies. This model has eight "white" and five black keys and correctly placed strings and pegs.

TABLE SETTING *(LEFT)*
Rather surprisingly, this table is from one of the bedrooms. It is set with fine porcelain and bone-handled cutlery on a delicate blue silk tablecloth, and is lit by a candle in a turned pewter candlestick with a twisted stem.

UTILITARIAN ITEMS

PERHAPS THE CHIEF GLORY of these fine old German houses lies in the original owners' insistence that the mundane is as worthy of being meticulously recorded in miniature as the exquisite. Indeed, it is usually those everyday items that viewers remember most vividly, as many such houses lack the magnificent collections of *objets d'art* found in Dutch and English examples. In the Stromer House, the display of metalwork in the kitchen is memorable, and items such as the tool-chest, with its fine assortment of miniature tools on top, are a joy.

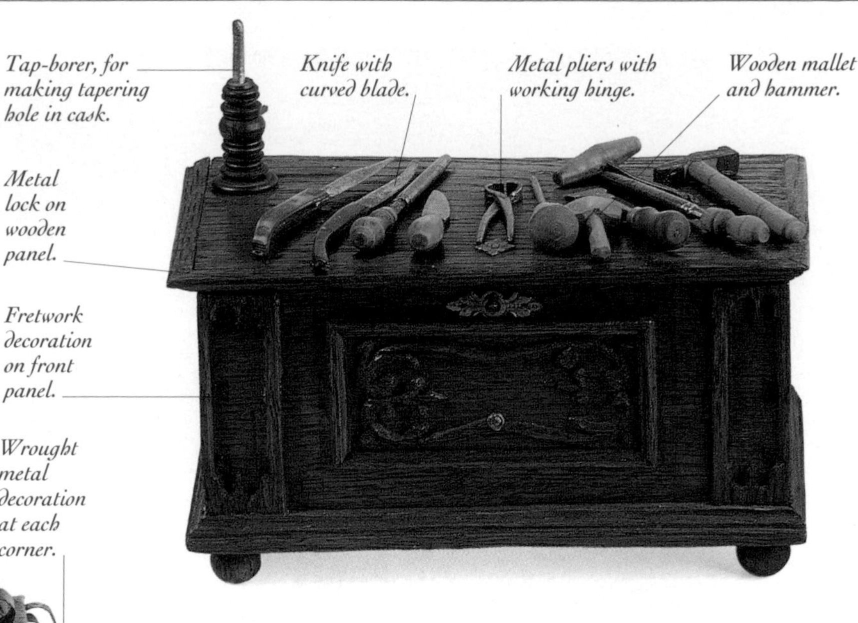

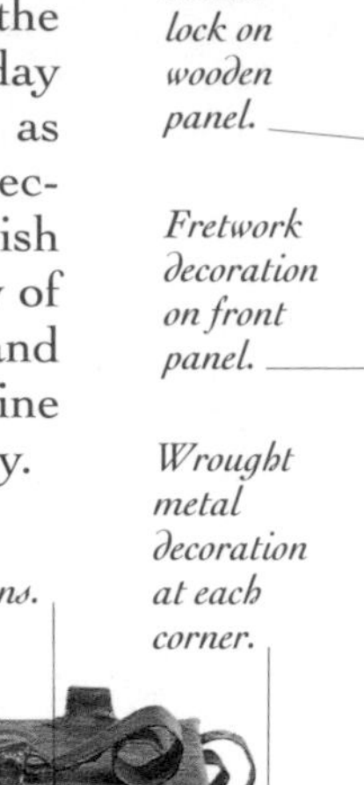

Plain wooden box painted red and green.

TOOL-CHEST *(ABOVE)* The importance of practical objects is underlined by placing this chest in a man-servant's bedroom, rather than in a store or workroom.

BABY CHAIR *(BELOW)* This baby chair, with a fretworked design on the back and sides, and a feeding-tray across the front, has no legs but is placed directly on the floor.

HAT-BOX AND CHEST *(ABOVE)* Plain wooden boxes, painted chests, and ornamental caskets are found in most of the rooms.

BABY-WALKER *(RIGHT)* Some baby-walkers were fixed to a post, which a child could encircle, but most were wheeled and untethered like this miniature model.

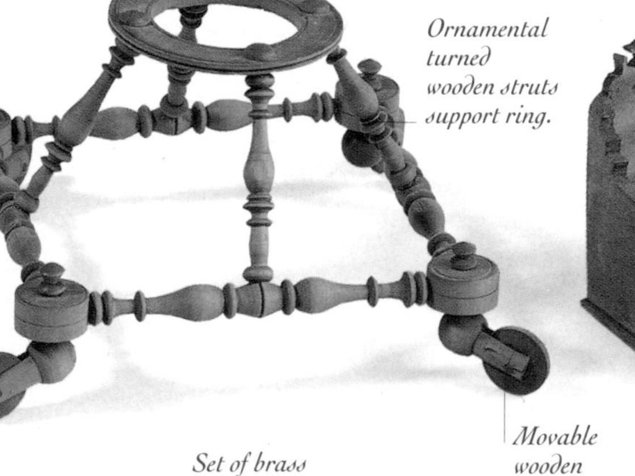

Carved wooden baby chair, with food-tray.

TABLE DESK *(BELOW)* This is a working table desk of plain black wood, where merchandise was weighed and listed, and deals were celebrated with a drink.

Pottery wine-jug.
Turned wooden candlestick.
Set of brass weights.
Sample of fleece.
Slate in wooden frame.
Wooden stool with three turned legs.
Metal hinge on cupboard door.

ACCOUNT BOOKS *(BELOW)* Heavy leather-bound ledgers such as these provided essential records of business transactions in seventeenth-century households.

Embossed leather cover of accounts book, dated 1640.
Indexed pages.
Leather-bound journal dated 1640.

Creel hanging from wall-hook.

Pewter plates kept in store-room.

Set of tankards on shelf.

Vegetable basket.

White-painted table with kitchen utensils.

Finely carved and painted horse, one of carriage pair.

Cow in individual stall.

Plain white-washed walls.

Wooden bedstead with fretwork panel on headboard.

Duvet and matching pillow in linen covers.

Towel-rail, holding linen towel.

Chess-board in green box.

Red and black tiled-effect floor.

Wooden tub on table.

Hessian sack, probably full of grain.

Black and white tiled floor.

Set of wooden trugs on floor.

Rack for barrels of beer and wine.

BREAD BASKET *(BELOW)* Baskets were indispensable, storing everything from linen to food, as well as being used to transport items about the house.

STOREROOM, BEDROOM, STABLE, AND CELLAR *(ABOVE)* These rooms reflect some practical aspects of maintaining a German townhouse in 1639: ample storage for stocks of food and drink was essential.

Willow basket containing home-made breads and rolls.

WOODEN COW *(RIGHT)* Like the two horses in neighbouring stalls, the cow has been realistically carved and painted with remarkable attention to anatomical detail.

Cow provides fresh milk for household.

DUTCH CABINET

Petronella de la Court; 1670–90

PETRONELLA DE LA COURT'S magnificent cabinet house is one of the oldest and finest in Holland; the cabinet itself, like other Dutch examples, is a handsome piece of furniture. A few alterations were made in the eighteenth century, and some silver had to be replaced after a theft in the nineteenth century. Otherwise the invaluable 1758 inventories ensure that everything is kept in its original place, giving an amazing insight into daily life in the home of a wealthy late-seventeenth-century merchant.

Petronella de la Court had many collections, of paintings, prints, porcelain, and precious stones, but she is best remembered for this sumptuously furnished cabinet house, commissioned in 1670, which took almost 20 years to complete.

Small entrance hall below entresol office.

207cm (81½in)

185cm (73in)

Olive-wood cabinet on "barley-sugar" twisted legs.

THE CABINET
The olive-wood cabinet is divided into 11 sections on three floors, representing rooms and a garden. The sides of the cabinet are decorated with a pattern of vertical and diagonal veneer strips.

Shelf holds row of lidded wooden jars.
Maid holds basket of game birds.
Slatted wall separates rooms.
Crystal chandelier with nine candles.
Wall covered by large oil painting.
Blue and white Delft-style plate.

Sumptuously furnished bedroom.
Brocade curtains and upholstery.
Wax doll wears silk brocade dress.
Maid looks after household laundry.
Maid irons laundry on trestle-table.
Wooden drying-rack suspended from ceiling.
Laundry list hangs on wall.

CENTRAAL MUSEUM, UTRECHT

SECOND FLOOR
On the left is a store-room, with a second store-room and maid's room behind the slats; next door is the nursery, then an elegant bedroom. On the far right is a laundry and linen-room.

FIRST FLOOR
This floor has two reception-rooms, one on either side of the low-ceilinged central hall, which has an entresol office above it. Such a room is often seen in seventeenth-century houses.

GROUND FLOOR
The doors in the back wall of the kitchen *(left)* lead to a cellar and a scullery. The lying-in room *(centre)* contains several ivory pieces, while the garden *(right)* has some fine ivory figures and a delicate ivory pavilion.

WORKS OF ART

DUTCH COLLECTORS in the seventeenth and eighteenth centuries used their cabinet houses as display cases for miniature *objets d'art* – though the houses also reflected life in their own homes. Possessing both wealth and taste, they created lavishly furnished examples, and their use of the costliest materials, including gold, silver, and ivory, distinguishes these houses from contemporary models in other countries. This magnificent house contains over 1,600 miniature items.

ARMCHAIR *(RIGHT)*
This brocade-upholstered chair is one of a set in the drawing-room. A wooden foot-warmer stands in front; heat from the smouldering charcoal escapes through the holes on top.

Arms and legs in "barley-sugar" twisted design.

Tasselled braid around upholstered seat.

Hinged door allows access to inside of foot-warmer.

Limewood foot-warmer holds imitation earthenware charcoal container.

Elaborate gilded frame.

Specially commissioned miniature work.

Artist's signature on back of oil painting.

RHINE LANDSCAPE *(ABOVE)*
Petronella de la Court commissioned both miniature and full-sized paintings from a number of well-known Dutch artists. This landscape, in an ornate gilt frame, is signed on the back by the artist Herman Saftleven, and dated 1678.

LINEN CUPBOARD *(RIGHT)*
The Dutch love of "hidden" treasures is not confined to miniature houses concealed within fine cabinets. A splendid trousseau of lace and linen is stored in this elaborate linen cupboard, with carved ivory figures in the door niches.

Carved ivory figure.

Biblical figure made of ivory; one of pair.

Linen cupboard filled with lace collars and linen.

Carved ivory relief represents "Faith".

Ivory relief represents "Hope".

"Barley-sugar" twisted legs.

COMPTOIR *(BELOW)*
Many seventeenth-century Dutch merchants' homes had a room like this, which served as an office. The well-to-do occupant wears an informal gown and slippers, possibly with a view to relaxing in the small room beyond the doorway in the back wall, which is furnished with a day-bed.

SKATES, RAT-TRAP, AND SPINNING-WHEEL *(BELOW/RIGHT)*
A pair of wooden skates is kept in the store-room, along with a rat-trap and this finely made spinning-wheel with ivory decoration.

Pair of wooden skates with string fastenings.

Large wood and metal rat-trap.

Carved ivory spindle.

Wooden spinning-wheel.

Letter addressed to "Heer Constantius Popperyus of Pouperys in't Poppe Húis".

Doorway to room with day-bed.

Shelves for account books.

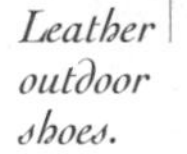

Leather outdoor shoes.

Informal brocaded-silk robe.

Comfortable slippers for indoor use.

Writing-desk with ink-well and quilled pen.

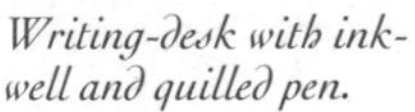

Well-stocked drinks case, with green glass flasks.

LONG-CASE CLOCK *(BELOW)*
The case of this beautiful clock, which has an English movement, is covered with tortoiseshell; it is decorated with gilded metal friezes and finials and has a small glazed inspection panel.

Lock with key in hinged front panel.

Clock perfectly balanced on marble base.

BOOKS AND GLOBE *(BELOW)* The globe shown is one of a pair, each mounted on an ebony stand, with brass meridian and longitudinal rings. The fine illustrated books are leather-bound, with gold-tooling.

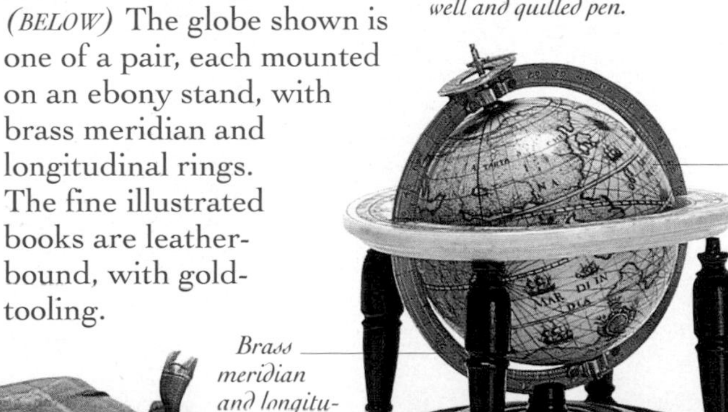

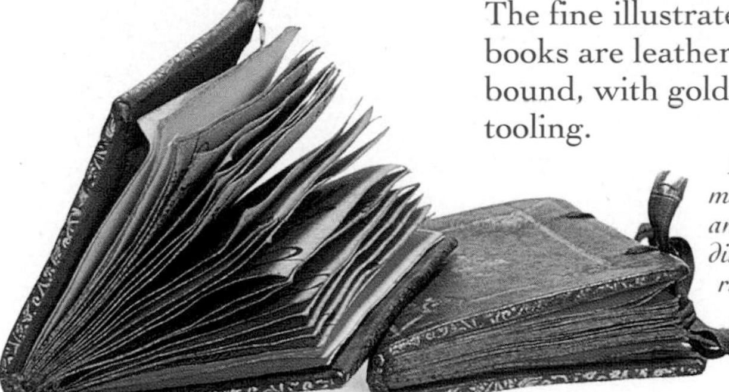

Leather-bound books illustrated with prints.

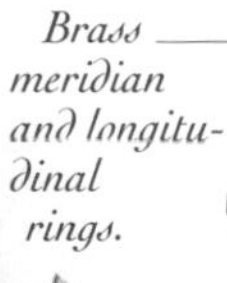

Brass meridian and longitudinal rings.

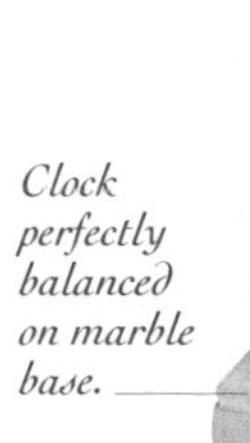

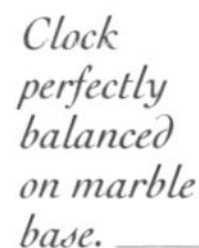

Finely painted terrestrial features.

WORK AND PLAY

ALTHOUGH DUTCH CABINET houses are renowned for their exquisite contents, their owners did not ignore the importance of utilitarian domestic items. To a researcher these miniature replicas, which so faithfully record the equipment used in seventeenth- and eighteenth-century kitchens, laundries, work-rooms, and even gardens, are as interesting and valuable as the more elaborate pieces that furnish the reception rooms.

FORMAL GARDEN *(BELOW)*
The garden is symmetrically laid out with a wonderful combination of practicality (fruit trees espaliered along walls, and in tubs), pleasure (flowers in beds, pots, and decorative urns), and fine art. The ivory statues are skilfully carved and match the delicate ivory arbour at the back of the garden.

LAUNDRY EQUIPMENT *(BELOW)*
The laundry is furnished with a linen-press filled with folded linen, a wooden tray of freshly laundered items, and a mousetrap. The two irons are used for different types of work.

Handle turns to tighten screw, applying pressure to linen.

Pressed and aired woollen night-cap.

Clean, folded linen.

Heavy wooden leaf connected to turning screws.

Wooden carrying tray.

Small trestle-table.

Thin plates placed between sheets to keep them flat.

Legs braced by two wooden struts.

Small iron, on heating stand, used for delicate fabrics.

Wood and metal multiple mousetrap.

Heavy iron, on stand, used for household linen.

Fruit trees line garden walls.

Exquisitely carved ivory statue representing one of four seasons.

Arbour constructed of delicate ivory rods.

Upper wall of garden section painted to represent sky.

Painted peacock on mural.

Rose bush with minute paper flowers in "terracotta" pot.

Small elderwood wheelbarrow provides utilitarian touch.

Seventeenth-century version of skittles carved in ivory.

Beautifully ornamented ivory urn holds fruit tree.

DUTCH WAX DOLLS

THE ENGLISH CONVENTION that wax dolls were used to represent the upper classes in society, leather the middle classes, and wood the lower classes, did not apply in Holland. In this house all the dolls have wax arms and heads with well-moulded, life-like faces. Although the limbs are padded and wired, enabling arms to hold different positions, the dolls' bodies are designed to stand, so those that have been placed in chairs look uncomfortably rigid. As the farmer doll has an identical twin in another house (in Amsterdam's Rijksmuseum), it is likely that some of the dolls were bought, not commissioned.

STAFF *(LEFT)*
As the servants in the cabinet house wear the regional costume of Vatersland, it is possible that the de la Court family had a connection with that district. The child (one of the family) wears a lace dress.

FAMILY *(BELOW)*
The dolls in the cabinet house are fashionably dressed in the Parisian styles that were worn in Holland in the 1680s and 90s. Some costumes, and particularly the womens' head-dresses, are very elaborate, with lace featuring predominantly.

Nursemaid wears regional costume.

Well-moulded wax face with vivacious expression.

Costume worn by farmers in Vatersland region of Holland.

Wide baggy trousers.

Leading-reins used to guide young child's steps.

Small child dressed as miniature adult.

Elaborate fontange *adorns lady's head.*

Wax doll's face may be "portrait" head, resembling a known person.

Full-bottomed wig worn by musician.

Red velvet coat, richly trimmed with gold buttons and braid.

Lace lappets arranged to frame wearer's face.

Miniature replica violin.

Beautiful lace jabot.

Apron trimmed with home-made lace.

Music stand with "barley-sugar" twisted support.

Ornate 1680s–90s costume.

CUPBOARD HOUSE

German; second half of seventeenth century

ALTHOUGH HOLLAND is the country that immediately springs to mind when thinking of cabinet houses, there are some notable early German examples. The German rooms, however, were usually housed in cupboards, the difference between cabinet and cupboard houses being not so much in their contents as in the structures that contain the rooms: cabinets are generally fine, decorative pieces of furniture, while cupboards are usually simple, functional containers. But the outward appearance of this German example – a plain, one-shelved cupboard with a panelled drawer in the base – belies the fine quality and exquisite detail of the furnishings and contents contained in the two rooms, arranged as a bed-sitting-room and kitchen.

Plain varnished wooden cupboard.

THE FACADE
Apart from some moulding around the top, and a panelled drawer front, this simple cupboard, divided into two rooms, is unadorned.

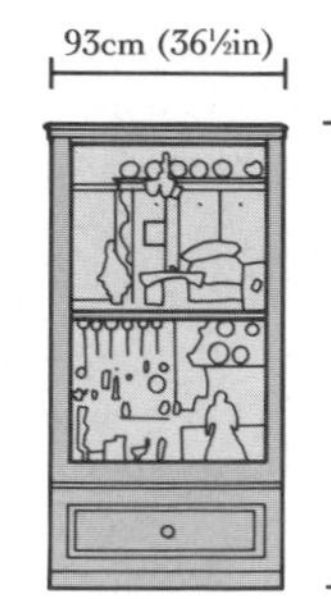

Varnished wooden cupboard with one shelf; drawer in base.

Shelves fill whole kitchen wall.

Hinged lid on pewter tankard.

Set of pewter plates on shelf.

Row of small, turned pewter mugs.

Large serving dish.

Low painted bench holds utilitarian items.

PEWTER DISPLAY *(ABOVE)*
The exceptional quality of this beautifully kept, eye-catching display of tableware and kitchen utensils testifies to the renowned skill of Nuremberg's metal workers.

Carved decorative edge on wooden panel.

Moulded figure on green glazed tile.

Metal semi-circular basin on fitted wash-stand.

Turned wooden leg on stand holding stove.

Upper Room

With the exception of the area just around the stove, the walls are panelled in natural wood with a decorative fretwork finish. The room is fully furnished with a sideboard, table, wash-stand, chest of drawers, and a bed in the corner, piled high with feather quilts. A six-branched brass candelabrum hangs from the ceiling.

Decorated dishes of blue and white Nuremberg faience on shelf.

Wood-chip paper pasted on wall behind stove.

Wire and wood bird-cage with feathered occupant.

Metal candle-snuffers hanging from hook.

Wooden stand for ceramic stove.

Plates stored and warmed on hood above hearth.

Skewers hooked onto spit.

Doll wears regional costume.

Ceramic Stove *(above)*

Many continental dolls' houses contain stoves, but few are of such fine quality as this ornate example, covered in intricately moulded, green glazed Nuremberg tiles. The stove is raised on a wooden stand, on a red and white tiled plinth.

Lower Room

With its exceptional display of pewter, wooden items, and kitchen equipment, this is one of the finest known early kitchens. The mechanical spit (dated 1550), the hallmarked, long-handled pans hanging on the back wall, and the wide range of cooking implements and utensils are not just individually valuable; as a detailed reference for the social historian they are priceless. The cook, with hair tied in two long braids, has unfortunately suffered serious damage to her wax face.

Germanisches National Museum, Nuremberg

FINE CRAFTSMANSHIP

ALL THE SMALLER accessories and household items are particularly well made: some of the spinning implements, for instance, are delicate miniature replicas. The larger pieces of furniture lack their fine finish, however; instead of veneer and carving, these pieces have varnish and fretwork decoration, and the favoured wood is pine. As this house, like the Stromer House *(see pp.18–23)*, is intended to reflect the home of a wealthy seventeenth-century German merchant, rather than a "stately home", the rooms and furnishings are entirely appropriate.

Ornamental fretwork on back of dresser.

One of pair of brass candlesticks.

Tiny pair of kid gloves on velvet-topped box.

Out-of-scale metal thimble.

Book hanging by long thread looped round hook.

Metal door handle and lock.

Moulding on base of cupboard matches that on bed.

CUPBOARD *(RIGHT)*
The decorative fretwork feature on the cupboard is similar to that on the bed and on the wooden panelling of the bed-sitting-room walls.

Brass double-eagle.

CHANDELIER *(ABOVE)*
Heavy miniature brass chandeliers, with varying numbers of branches for candles, are found in many dolls' houses. Few, though, would have had the double-headed Imperial Eagle for a decoration, as seen on this splendid German example.

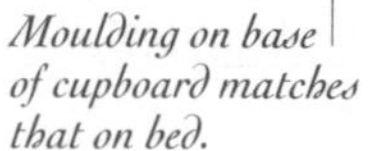

Small head-pillow with matching down-filled bolster.

Decorative, high wooden headboard.

Linen sheet with decorative tassels.

Top feather-filled duvet in white linen cover.

Middle duvet in blue and white checked cover.

Lowest duvet acts as soft mattress.

Straw-filled mattress laid on bed-base.

Metal bed-warmer.

Tiny pair of kid slippers with laces.

WOODEN BED *(RIGHT)*
Looking at the towering mass of bedding on many continental beds, it may seem an impossible feat for anyone to climb on top or burrow underneath such a mountainous pile – but once in bed, a body's weight made it sink slightly into true feather-bedded comfort.

MECHANICAL SPIT *(RIGHT)* This is one of the more sophisticated examples from a variety of spits found in seventeenth-century dolls' house kitchens. Its cog-wheel mechanism turns the skewer holding the meat near the fire on the hearth.

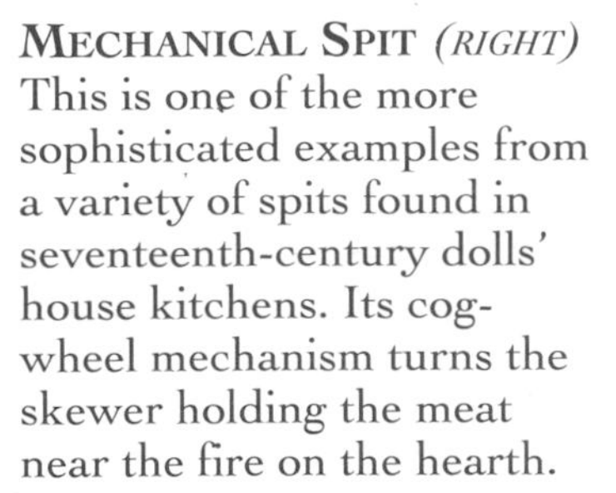

Metal spit with turning mechanism.

Holder for metal skewers.

Skewer in place on spit.

Broad tripod base to balance heavy spit.

Selection of skewers in different sizes.

PEWTER WARE *(BELOW)* The kitchen contains a wealth of pewter items, including this lidded pail with an embossed back-section, a teapot, and a kitchen syringe.

Decorative back on pewter pail.

Pewter teapot with bound handle.

Metal syringe.

WAX-FACED DOLL

LIKE THE OTHER TWO occupants of the house, this doll has a stuffed fabric body with waxed face and hands, a wig, and beautifully made clothes. He wears a black full-skirted coat with gathered lace jabot and lace-edged shirt cuffs – all in remarkable condition given their age.

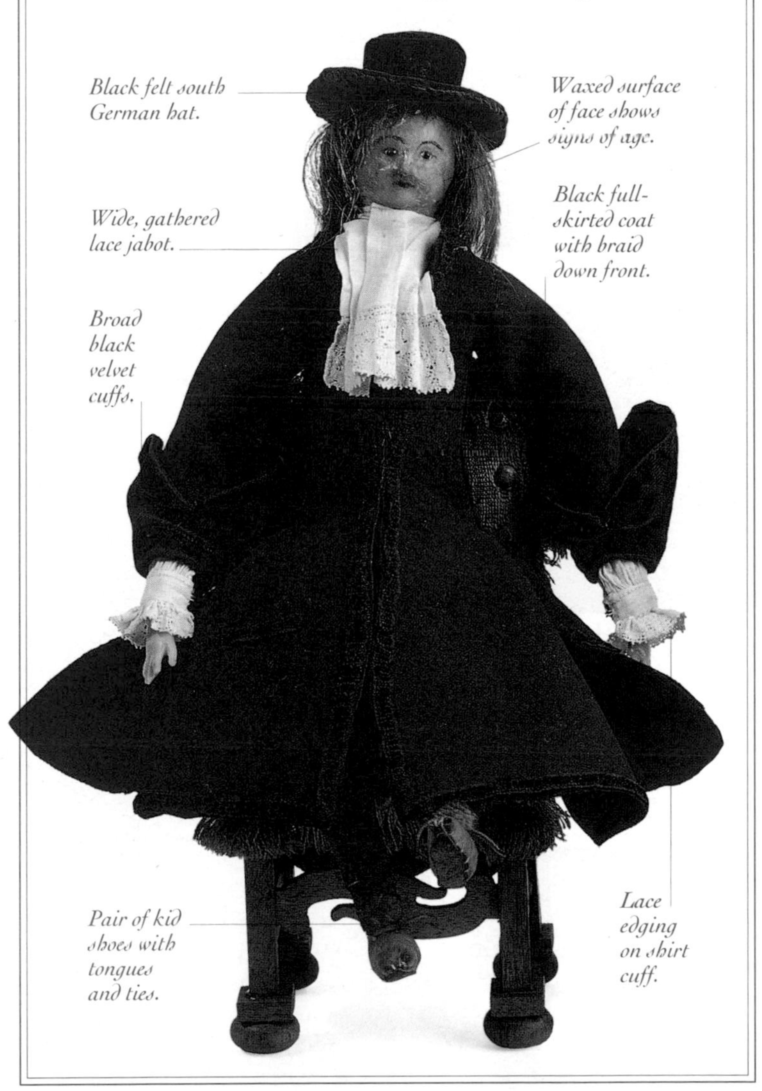

Black felt south German hat.

Waxed surface of face shows signs of age.

Wide, gathered lace jabot.

Black full-skirted coat with braid down front.

Broad black velvet cuffs.

Pair of kid shoes with tongues and ties.

Lace edging on shirt cuff.

SPINDLE AND LACE-MAKER *(LEFT)* Spinning, weaving, and lace-making were important activities in many seventeenth-century households, and this is reflected in the detail on these beautifully made miniature replicas of some of the associated tools and equipment.

Fleece impaled on holder ready for spinning.

Highly decorative stand with arms to hold wooden spindles.

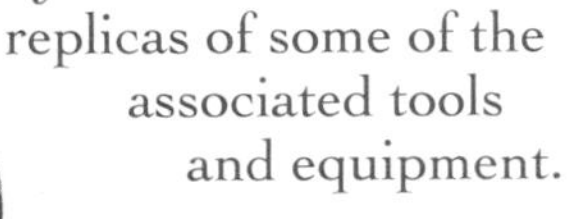

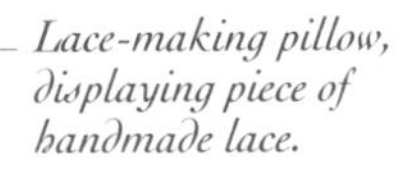

Lace-making pillow, displaying piece of handmade lace.

Delicately turned lace-pillow-stand with tripod legs.

CHOPPING BLOCK AND PLATE-CARRIER *(BELOW)* Kitchen implements in affluent seventeenth-century homes, usually made of wood, were often decorative.

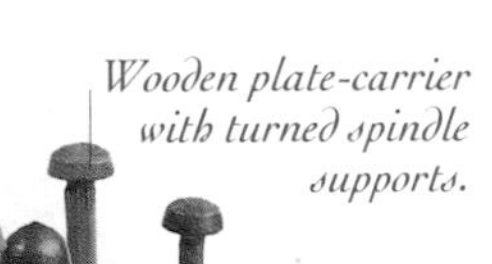

Wooden plate-carrier with turned spindle supports.

Maplewood plates for everyday use.

Wooden chopping-block with three turned legs.

Butcher's axe with wooden handle and metal blade.

MINIATURE REALISM

SARA PLOOS VAN AMSTEL was a meticulous recorder who kept invaluable inventories, recording dates, makers, and often the cost of her purchases. With 250 items in the kitchen alone, and fine examples of miniature *objets d'art* in every room, this house is a collector's dream. Particularly noteworthy is the collection of miniature Dutch silver, much of it commissioned from well-known silversmiths such as Arnoldus van Geffen and Jan Borduur.

CLAVICHORD *(RIGHT)*
Music was an important entertainment in eighteenth-century homes; several family members would have been talented amateur musicians. This is a beautiful replica of a popular instrument of the period.

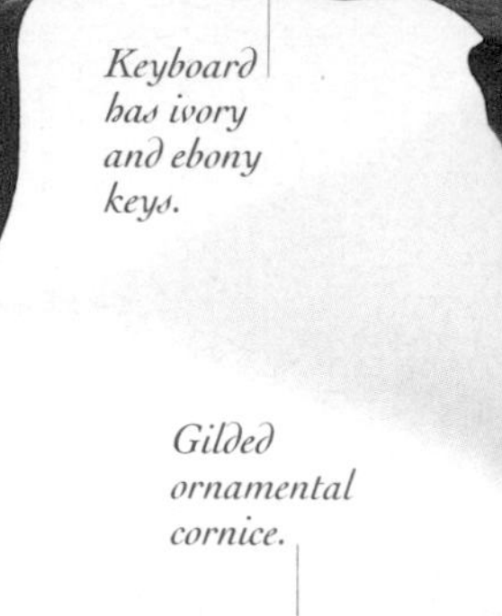

Strings and pegs.

Keyboard has ivory and ebony keys.

Mid-eighteenth-century-style clavichord with cabriole legs.

CARD-TABLE *(RIGHT)*
The flower design on the cover of this card-table was embroidered by Sara in silks on satin. The cover is edged with braid to fit neatly over the table's octagonal edges.

Octagonal wooden table with tilting top.

Hand-embroidered table cover.

Carved tripod legs.

LINEN CUPBOARD *(BELOW)*
This fine linen cupboard resembles the full-scale cabinet containing Sara Ploos van Amsel's first miniature house, which is now in a museum in The Hague.

Miniature porcelain vase.

Each section holds a different set of linen.

Walnut-veneered, serpentine-front linen cupboard.

Ornate metal door handle.

Drawer filled with linen and lace.

PAINTED PANEL *(RIGHT)*
The delicate gold and red decoration on the mouldings of this panel are not original, but were over-painted in the nineteenth century.

Gilded ornamental cornice.

Naturalistic flower painting possibly by Jurriaan Buttner.

Stylized panel, over-painted in nineteenth century.

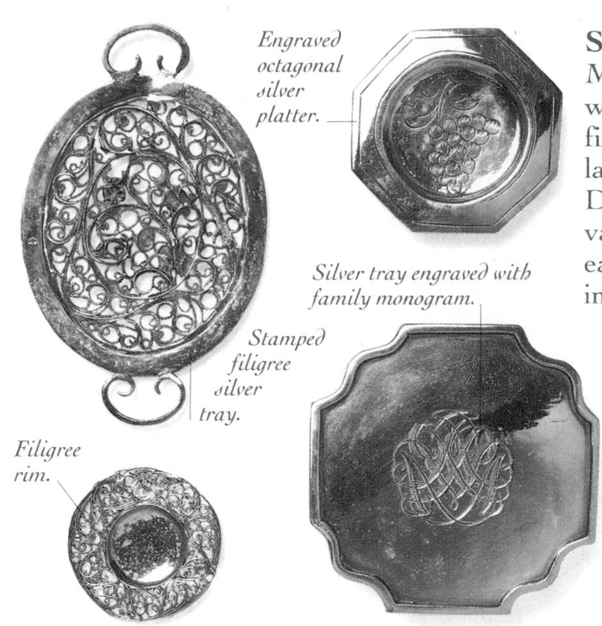

SILVERWARE *(LEFT)* Much of the fine silverware, including the two filigree pieces here, is late seventeenth-century Dutch, but Sara Ploos van Amstel also had earlier examples in her impressive collection.

COLLECTOR'S CABINET *(RIGHT)* This intriguing late-seventeenth-century ebony-veneered cabinet, with working lock and metal decoration, contains a miniature collection of coral and tiny shells.

Copper corner decoration.

Carrying handle set into top panel.

Small drawer holds minute shell collection.

Key in working metal lock.

Perfectly balanced legs and stretchers.

MID-EIGHTEENTH-CENTURY WAX DOLLS

THE DIMINUTIVE GIRL DOLL, with her old-fashioned high *fontange*, the nurse, and the reclining male doll all have realistically moulded and painted wax heads; the dolls' costumes are typical of those worn in the mid-eighteenth century by the characters they represent. According to fascinating notebooks that were kept by Sara Ploos van Amstel, she and her cousin, Nicht Hoogehuyse, dressed a few of the dolls in the house. Most, however, were bought then redressed especially for Sara by a Frenchman named Jac Castang. The nurse's bonnet, daintily patterned apron, and dress are plainer, cheaper, and rather old-fashioned versions of a lady's costume. The householder prefers comfort to fashion, judging by his warm brocaded house-gown, knitted woollen cap and stockings, and heavy shoes.

TIFFANY-PLATT

American; made c.1860

WHEN FLORA GILL JACOBS acquired this dolls' house in 1957, it was known as the Tiffany House, in the belief that it had been made for a member of the Tiffany family. Subsequent research revealed that a previous owner bought it at a sale of the Platt family's possessions, and so Mrs Jacobs renamed it the Tiffany-Platt House.

Behind the imposing facade of this splendid detached New York brownstone are several fine rooms but, although the two top rooms and those on the ground floor have connecting doors, there are no stairs linking them with the drawing-room. Although the location of the dining-room on the top floor may seem improbable, it was placed like this when Mrs Jacobs acquired the house, and she decided that the room was too elegant to move to the low-ceilinged "basement".

Framed three-dimensional Valentine.

Painted metal wash-stand with toilet set.

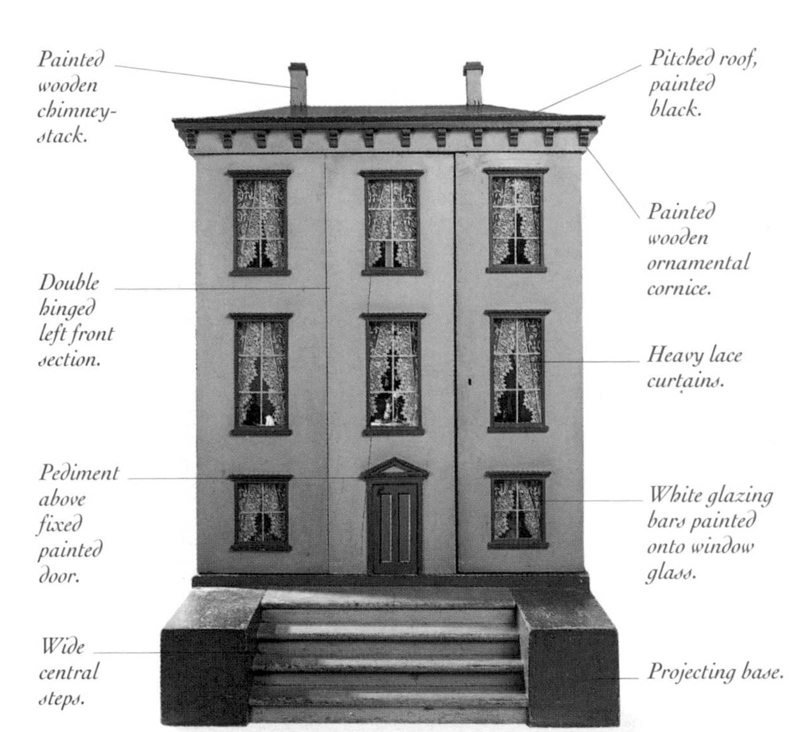

Heavy gilded metal display cabinet with porcelain collection.

One of two side windows.

Black-haired china doll holds paper fan.

Ormolu-framed rocking chair with rose-coloured upholstery on seat.

Bisque nanny doll in original uniform.

"Frozen Charlotte" china baby doll in rocking cradle.

Red-stained chair with fringed, upholstered seat.

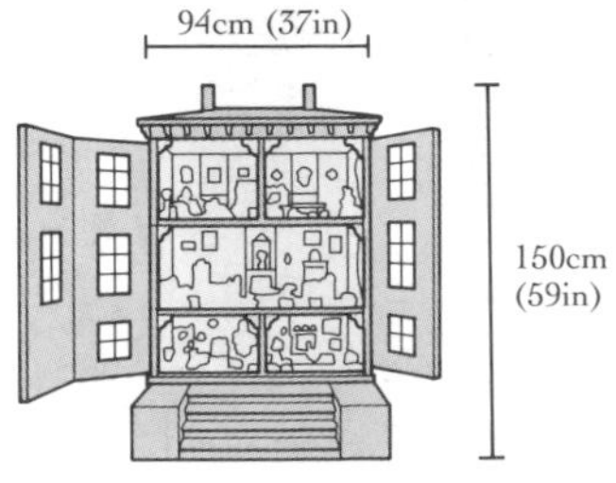

Painted wooden structure; hinged three-section facade; raised base.

THE FACADE
The relatively small ground-floor windows on this mid-nineteenth-century New York townhouse give it a rather foreshortened appearance; this is accentuated by the outsize front steps on the projecting base, which may have been designed to provide seating for children.

SECOND FLOOR
The rooms on this floor are arranged as a bedroom *(left)* and, oddly, a dining-room *(right)*. The dining-room contains wood, marble, and gilded metal pieces. In the bedroom, personal possessions include a hat-box and a gilt work-box.

Gilded pressed metal electric light sconce.

Dark wood jardinière *with pots of fabric plants.*

FIRST FLOOR
The drawing-room, which occupies the whole first floor, is especially well lit by seven high windows and numerous lights. The many delicate gilt items also help to lighten this elegant room, and provide a contrast to the dark wooden furniture.

Student's (or library) lamp on bureau.

Gilded metal "tête-à-tête" chairs with silk seats.

Velvet dog and puppies on felt rug.

GROUND FLOOR
The kitchen *(right)* is fully equipped, with items ranging from a metal mangle to a set of muffin-moulds. The room next door contains a set of red stained wooden furniture and several gilded metal pieces.

WASHINGTON DOLLS' HOUSE & TOY MUSEUM

ELEGANT RELAXATION

THE TIFFANY-PLATT HOUSE evokes nostalgia for a bygone, pre-plastic age – a time when dolls' house furniture was made of metal, wood, or cardboard, and dolls were of china, bisque, or composition. It also illustrates the pride taken in creating stylish, comfortable homes that characterized the late-nineteenth-century period. An added delight is the fact that so many of the pieces in the house are still in their original condition; even if sometimes a trifle faded or worn, this merely emphasizes their quality.

FOUR-POSTER BED *(RIGHT)*
From its draught-excluding top to its carved sides, this Waltershausen bed promises warmth and relaxation; the braided pelmet and lace-trimmed pink silk curtains and bed-cover enhance the effect. The bed-warmer and chamber-pot provide utilitarian comfort.

Decorative finial at each corner.

Wooden top on Waltershausen four-poster bed.

Original lace-trimmed silk curtains.

Lace over silk bedspread is original.

Gilt transfer imitates inlay on rosewood.

Metal hot-water bed-warmer.

China chamber-pot.

METAL BED *(BELOW)*
The crimson bedspread sets off very effectively the gilt tracery on the sides and ends of this late-nineteenth-century metal bed, with its elaborate head and foot panels.

Decorative bed-head.

Gilded pierced-metal side panel.

Ornate, gilded metal single bed.

Crimson bedspread covers deep mattress.

SOFA AND CHAIRS *(BELOW)*
As well as the sofa and two chairs shown here, the set of furniture in the nursery includes a dressing-table and mirror, all in the same dark red stained wood. The lace-covered cushion on the sofa is trimmed with red ribbon.

Wooden chair stained dark red.

Rocking-chair upholstered in star-patterned fabric.

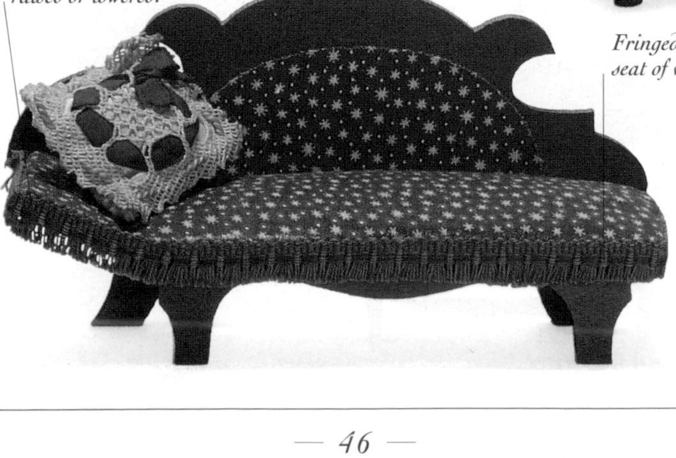

Arm-rest can be raised or lowered.

Fringed red braid around seat of wooden sofa.

LAMP *(LEFT)*
This fine miniature version of a popular full-scale table-lamp has a pink glass globe around its clear glass chimney.

Table-lamp with gilt base.

WELL-DRESSED DOLLS

ALL THE DOLLS in the Tiffany-Platt house, which has 11 occupants as well as household pets, wear well-made distinctive period costumes: the staff's uniform was commercially made, but the other dolls' clothes may have been hand-made. Most of the dolls, including the nanny and the child, have bisque heads and wired, soft bodies, but the other three adult dolls on this page have composition heads and hands. Like most American dolls' house dolls, they are "immigrants", imported from Germany and France.

NANNY AND BABY *(LEFT)*
Nanny, dressed in a simple brown dress and white lace-trimmed apron, has a bisque head. The tiny unclothed baby doll in the cradle is a "Frozen Charlotte", made of glazed china. Both dolls were manufactured in Germany.

DOGS *(LEFT)*
The bitch and her three puppies are made of wrinkled brown velvet; the white dog is ceramic.

CHILD AND ADULTS *(RIGHT)*
The child is a jointed bisque doll, while the adults must be visitors as they, alone of all the dolls in the house, have wired, soft bodies with painted composition heads and hands.

GEORGIAN HOUSE

English; made by John Hodgson; 1991

THE GEORGIAN HOUSE was the second house that John Hodgson created for the Guthrie Collection at Hever Castle, Edenbridge, Kent, England (the first was a medieval house, the latest is Stuart). Initially conceived as an exhibition of miniature room sets, the collection developed into a uniquely presented display housed in 1:12 scale models, with cut-away sections in the walls revealing specifically chosen rooms.

The Georgian House, based on Palladian-style architecture, is made of painted fibreboard, with fine woods used for the internal doors and furniture. Many features and furnishings were inspired by those at Sledmere House, in Yorkshire, England. Several well-known British miniaturists also contributed items to this outstanding example of contemporary craftsmanship.

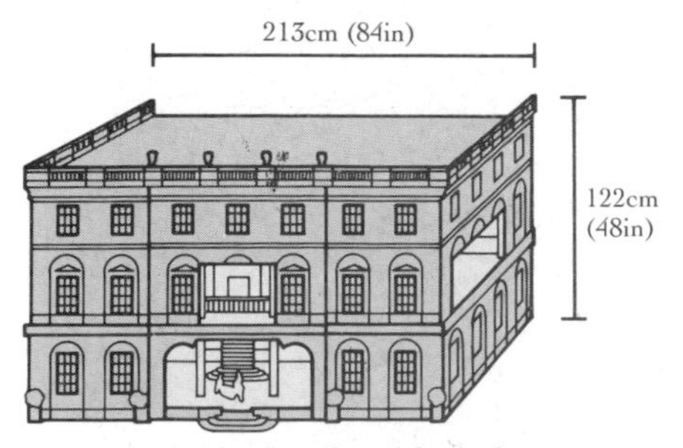

Painted fibreboard; solid wood doors; fixed, glazed sash-windows; open sections on three sides.

THE LIBRARY *(ABOVE)*
Details such as the small carpet, embroidered by Patricia Borwick, and the crystal chandelier by Donald Ward contribute to this exquisite recreation of a Georgian interior with its "Chippendale" chairs, partners' desk, and tables of wood and gilt. Three figures are grouped around a flickering fire, created with the aid of fibre-optics by Keith Evans, who designed all the lighting in the house.

Blind of coloured card fixed behind top-floor window.

Open section reveals library, above drawing-room, on right side of house.

Dining-room table visible through front sash window.

Gravel around base of house.

Classical urn on balustrade.

Solid pillar between sections of turned balusters.

Nine-paned sash-window fixed in position.

Head of rain-water pipe initialled "J.H. 1991".

Modillion-style moulding under cornice.

TOP FLOOR
There is no cut-away section on the top floor, but the positions of the sash windows and their blinds have been varied to give it a lived-in appearance.

Pedimented window-frame set in recessed arched alcove.

FIRST FLOOR
The beautifully framed cut-away section reveals "marble" columns, gilded filigree balusters, and an imposing portrait of Lady Eglington – a miniature oil painting copied from the original by Reynolds.

Ornamental "stonework" on recessed arch around sash window.

GROUND FLOOR
In the entrance hall, which is furnished with gilded metal pieces, two footmen struggle to carry a trunk past the marbled columns, up the grand staircase.

Flower-filled "stone" urn on pedestal.

Solid mahogany door to dining-room.

Curved flight of steps painted to resemble stone.

Black and white tiled hall floor.

Gilded bronze hall-table.

Wall grooved to imitate stonework.

MODERN MINIATURES

THE GEORGIAN HOUSE contains many excellent examples of modern miniaturists' artistry and skill. John Hodgson's beautifully designed and constructed chairs (some of wood, others of gilded cast bronze) are particularly memorable. Also impressive is Karen Griffith's exquisite, hand-made 1:12 scale "Wedgwood" bone-china dinner service, with a Greek key motif. Each piece bears the monogram "G" for Guthrie.

MODEL SHIP *(ABOVE)*
Made by Paul Briggs, this model is a meticulously reproduced replica of the *Golden Hind*, the ship in which Sir Francis Drake became the first English person to circumnavigate the world (1577–80).

TABLE AND CHAIR *(ABOVE)*
John Hodgson designed both the Georgian-style table and the chair, which displays intricate moulding, including masks on the "knees". The pieces were cast in bronze then gilded.

TORCHERE *(ABOVE)*
This imposing gilded bronze torchère, one of a pair in the hall, holds a five-branched candelabrum. It was made by John Hodgson.

Filigree-metal decoration around clock-handle.

Battery-operated hands on working clock.

BRACKET CLOCK *(ABOVE)*
Ken Palmer made this fine clock in an ebonized case.

DESK AND CHAIR *(ABOVE)*
With four pedestals front and back, containing drawers or cupboards, this is a model of a partners' desk. Alongside is a mahogany Chippendale-style chair with ribbon back and claw and ball feet.

DINING TABLE *(BELOW)*
John Hodgson's mahogany dining table, laden with "Georgian" silver and fine porcelain, is complemented by his set of Chippendale-style chairs. The silverware is by Stuart McCabe, Josie Studd, and Ken Palmer, and glassware by Edward Hall.

Painted cast-iron dish with moulded flower decoration.

Mahogany table on four, four-legged pedestals.

MODELLED FIGURINE

ALL THE FIGURES in the house – including the servants in the hall, members of the family in the library, and a music master in the drawing-room – were made by David Hoyle. Modelled in Milliput then painted, their costumes reflect the fashions of eighteenth-century England. John Hodgson chose modelled figurines for the Georgian House as they can be posed in more realistic positions than dolls' house dolls.

SHOPS, SCHOOLS, AND ROOM SETS

Although the basic shape of most shops, schools, and room sets might be described as "just three sides and a base", within these simple confines you will find some of the most fascinating scenes imaginable. They have been made for centuries, all over Europe and in the Americas, for a variety of purposes, including religious and secular education. Today, the popularity of such settings among collectors is as wide as their range.

ROOM SETS have a long and ancient history, as discoveries in ancient Greek, Roman, and Egyptian tombs testify. They have been used for a number of different purposes over the years: as playthings, as *objets d'art,* or as funeral artefacts, chosen to accompany the dead into their next life. The Greek philosopher Plato once suggested that miniature rooms have an educational function, helping to arouse the interest of boys in building and that of girls in housewifery; Plato's views were often regarded as controversial, however, so it is very unlikely that educational room sets were common in ancient Greece. In the Mediterranean countries, room sets seem to have been created almost exclusively for religious purposes, with Christmas Cribs being the most usual example.

Further north, in Europe, room sets had a more secular use. In Germany, particularly, mothers used them to help teach their young daughters the

BUTCHER'S SHOP *(LEFT)*
A plaque inscribed "Milligans, Dumfries, 1843" on the facade of this splendid butcher's shop commemorates a real-life family who have been butchers in Scotland since 1820.

FOLDING ROOM *(ABOVE)*
The trompe l'oeil *on the back wall of this room is particularly effective and illustrates the high quality of printing on German lithographed room sets in the late nineteenth century.*

PERUVIAN SHOP *(RIGHT)*
Exuberantly painted in traditional Peruvian folk-art style, this little wooden shop positively glows. It was made and painted by I. Lopez of Aurocucho, Peru, and contains seven modelled figures and a profusion of fabrics and hats that hang on the walls and spill over the counter.

housewifery skills they would require in adult life. Miniature kitchens were especially popular, and a number of examples exist that date from the mid-seventeenth century onwards. So-called Nuremberg kitchens became famous throughout Europe, although kitchens were also made in Augsburg, another German toy-making centre.

The tiny utensils crafted for these kitchens in ceramic and silver, and in other less precious metals, attracted the attention of collectors, who added some particularly fine examples to the collections of decorative miniature reception rooms that were so popular during the nineteenth century.

— Modern Collectables —

Although American and British collectors have traditionally preferred dolls' houses, they have never ignored room settings. Indeed many modern collectors now prefer room sets to dolls' houses because they take up less display space. Two superb examples are the French Parlour exhibited in Flora Gill Jacob's Washington Dolls' House and Toy Museum *(see pp.60–61)*, and the two-room setting with Rock & Graner furniture from a private collection in England *(see pp.64–65)*. Twentieth-century collectors have added bathrooms to their displays of room sets; painted tin examples with complex plumbing systems are now attracting increasing attention *(see pp.70–71)*. (Modern plastic versions are beginning to appear in the shops for popular dolls, such as Barbie, who already have everything else they need.)

A growing trend among both amateur and professional artist-craftsmen is to produce fully equipped, miniature workshops; toy and dolls' house makers' studios are predictable favourites. On a similar theme, a friend of mine made the fascinating, 1930s-style Veterinary Surgery *(see p.55)* to commemorate her husband's profession.

Even cheap and cheerful twentieth-century toy rooms, which were originally manufactured as playthings for children, are now extremely collectable. The small, three-walled tin-plate rooms that

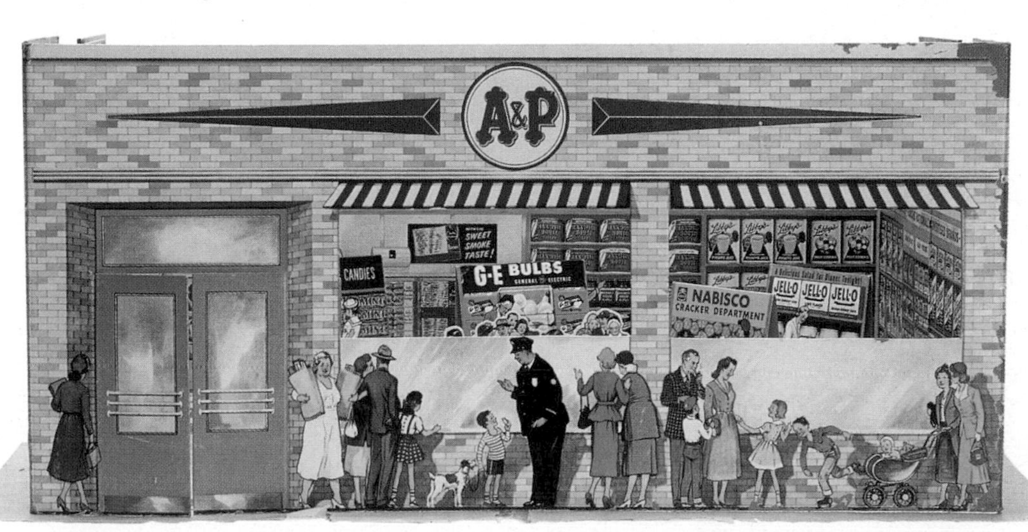

A & P STORE *(LEFT)*
Part of a 1940s promotion for an early American supermarket (Atlantic & Pacific), this store provided the basis for a children's game. Posters on the walls also urged its customers to invest in US defence bonds.

MARX ROOMS *(RIGHT)*
The 1920s American toy manufacturer, Louis Marx, produced two series of lithographed tin rooms – the Newlywed set, and these examples from the Home Town series, which included stores and other buildings. Each set contained six rooms.

were produced by the American firm Louis Marx, and sold at pocket-money prices by Woolworths and similar stores in the 1920s, now attract the attention of collectors at auction.

— MINIATURE EXTRAVAGANZA —

Three women who indulged their enthusiasm for miniatures beyond most collectors' wildest dreams have each left fascinating and illuminating records for others to admire and study. In 1704 Princess Augusta Dorothea von Schwarzburg-Arnstadt began work on Mon Plaisir, a miniature complex that replicated her court, the town, and surrounding countryside, peopled with 400 dolls dressed to represent all strata of society. Mon Plaisir bankrupted Princess Augusta Dorothea, who died in 1751, but social historians, costume researchers, and all who appreciate miniature artistry owe her a debt that can never be repaid.

During the 1920s, two other women – Mrs Narcissa Thorne (*née* Niblack), an American, and Mrs Katherine Carlisle (*née* Apcar) in England – each created a series of rooms recording interior decoration over the centuries. Both commissioned the finest craftsmen and artists to furnish their rooms, but there the similarity ends: Mrs Thorne's rooms, now displayed in Chicago's Art Institute, were created for educational purposes; Mrs Carlisle's rooms, which were bequeathed to the English National Trust, were personal records and reflect her life-long love of fine needlework.

— INTERNATIONAL SHOPPING —

Miniature shops have long been popular: early versions were often market-stalls but, by 1800, both shops and stalls were common German toys. By the beginning of the twentieth century, every kind of shop was being made in the main toy-

SCHOOLROOM *(LEFT)*
A nun, dressed in black habit, teaches this class of attentive, neatly uniformed pupils in a Spanish convent school. The room, complete with desks and wall charts, folds up into the box that constitutes the walls.

producing countries. Each one had its specialities: England was famous for its butchers' shops, and the United States for the use of lithographed wood and paper-board. The Milliner's Shop *(see pp.66–67)* is typical of the lavishly decorated shops made in Germany and France.

Printed cardboard shops and stores were popular playthings, as they were both colourful and cheap. Post-offices came with stamps and telegrams, drapers' shops with bolts of fabric – and, for less than the cost of one fine wooden example, you could have a whole street of shops.

Several South American countries are now well known for their cheerfully decorated pottery examples and, over the years, both China and Japan have produced detailed miniature stalls and shops stocked with a wide variety of tiny goods.

— LEARNING IS FUN —

Schoolrooms were also produced – some as teaching toys (one delightful Spanish schoolroom has 26 pupils representing alphabet letters), while others, in elaborately equipped settings, appealed to adults as collector's items. The best-known examples were produced in Europe, their pupils and teachers usually French or German wooden or bisque dolls, provided with books, slates, and maps. There are examples from other parts of the world, however: one schoolroom in my collection is the engaging *c.*1890 Japanese class *(see p.12)*, all seated on bamboo chairs and dressed in traditional *kimonos*. Modern versions of schools are rare, but both individual craftsmen and manufacturing companies are still producing shops and room-settings made of wood, cardboard, or plastic. There are also many do-it-yourself kits and cut-out books on the market that make up into perfectly satisfactory settings.

NUREMBERG COOK BOOK *(RIGHT)*
A rare treasure from the Washington Dolls' House & Toy Museum is this tiny book, which was printed in Nuremberg in 1858. The cover illustration shows that miniature kitchens were playthings as well as teaching toys.

Whether simple and cheap, or created by artists and craftsmen as specially commissioned orders, room sets, in all their variety, have retained their popularity over the centuries, and seem highly likely to go on doing so for many years to come.

VETERINARY SURGERY *(BELOW)*
This delightfully evocative two-room-setting was created by the English owner as a souvenir of her husband's veterinary surgery in the 1930s. Among the rooms' contents are a tray of minuscule medical instruments and several waiting patients.

GERMAN KITCHEN

Nuremberg kitchen; made in Germany c.1800

TEACHING BY MEANS OF "SHOW AND TELL" sessions has, for centuries, provided a valuable method of imparting information to children. Traditionally, and particularly in Germany, mothers have instructed their daughters in housekeeping skills. This *c.*1800 Nuremberg kitchen was designed specifically as an aid to educating girls for the roles assigned to them in adult life at that time. Room-settings, rather than complete houses, have always been favoured for educational purposes in Europe, and kitchens were produced in quantity. Designs for these ranged from a simple box-like room, with a painted hearth and a few pots and pans, to elaborate settings fitted with carved chimney-pieces, glazed cupboards, and shelves weighed down with crockery, pots, and cooking implements – and including, of course, a cook.

THE KITCHEN
Because the toy kitchen is a teaching aid, the contents are considered to be more important than the structure of the room itself. However, most kitchens are equipped with hearths with chimney-pieces, shelves, and wall-hooks. This example, which is too early to boast a stove, has an open hearth; its fine chimney is both functional and ornamental.

Finely carved hair-style.

Well-painted character face.

Over-large hands typical of crib figures.

Cook wears embroidered apron.

COOK *(LEFT)*
With her life-like expression and posture, and well-made clothing, this doll came originally from a Christmas crib – a religious "educational aid" often found in southern Germany.

Side shelf holds pottery jugs and jars.

Pan hangs on wooden peg.

Tin-lined copper pan is one of set.

Tin scoop for flour or grain.

Polished pewter table candlestick.

Heavy turned brass cauldron.

Oval tin-lined copper container.

Paper floor-covering with printed pattern.

Barrel-shaped wooden storage jar with lid.

Chafing-dish stands on metal tripod with handle.

91cm (36in)

43cm (17in)

Painted wooden structure of back, sides, and floor.

IRON, LAMP, AND JUG *(ABOVE)* These items, all realistic miniature replicas, are typical of those found in a well-equipped, eighteenth-century kitchen. The iron is specifically shaped for pressing sleeves.

CHOPPING BLOCK *(RIGHT)* The three-legged wooden block provides Cook with a strong base for chopping wood for the fire, or cutting up meat. On the block are an axe and a two-handled cutter with curved blade.

WASHINGTON DOLLS' HOUSE & TOY MUSEUM

SCHOOL EQUIPMENT *(RIGHT)* The wooden desks, with opening lids and fixed seats, were all in the schoolroom originally, along with the blackboard. The tiny cardboard slates, the school bell, and the exercise books, with marbled-paper covers, all made in Germany, were later additions.

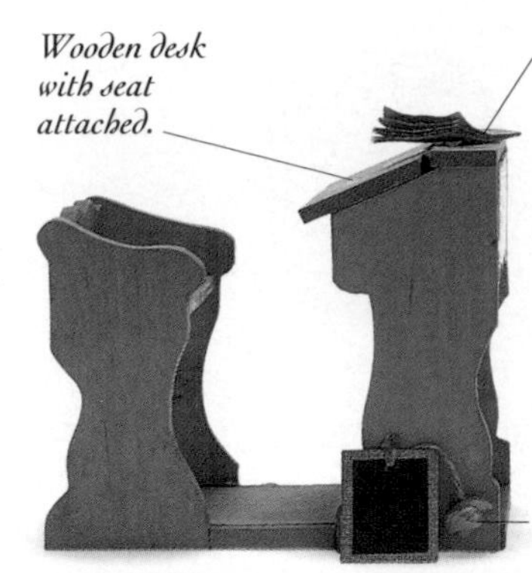

Wooden desk with seat attached.

Exercise book with marbled cover.

Sponge for wiping slate, attached by string.

Pegs secure blackboard to easel.

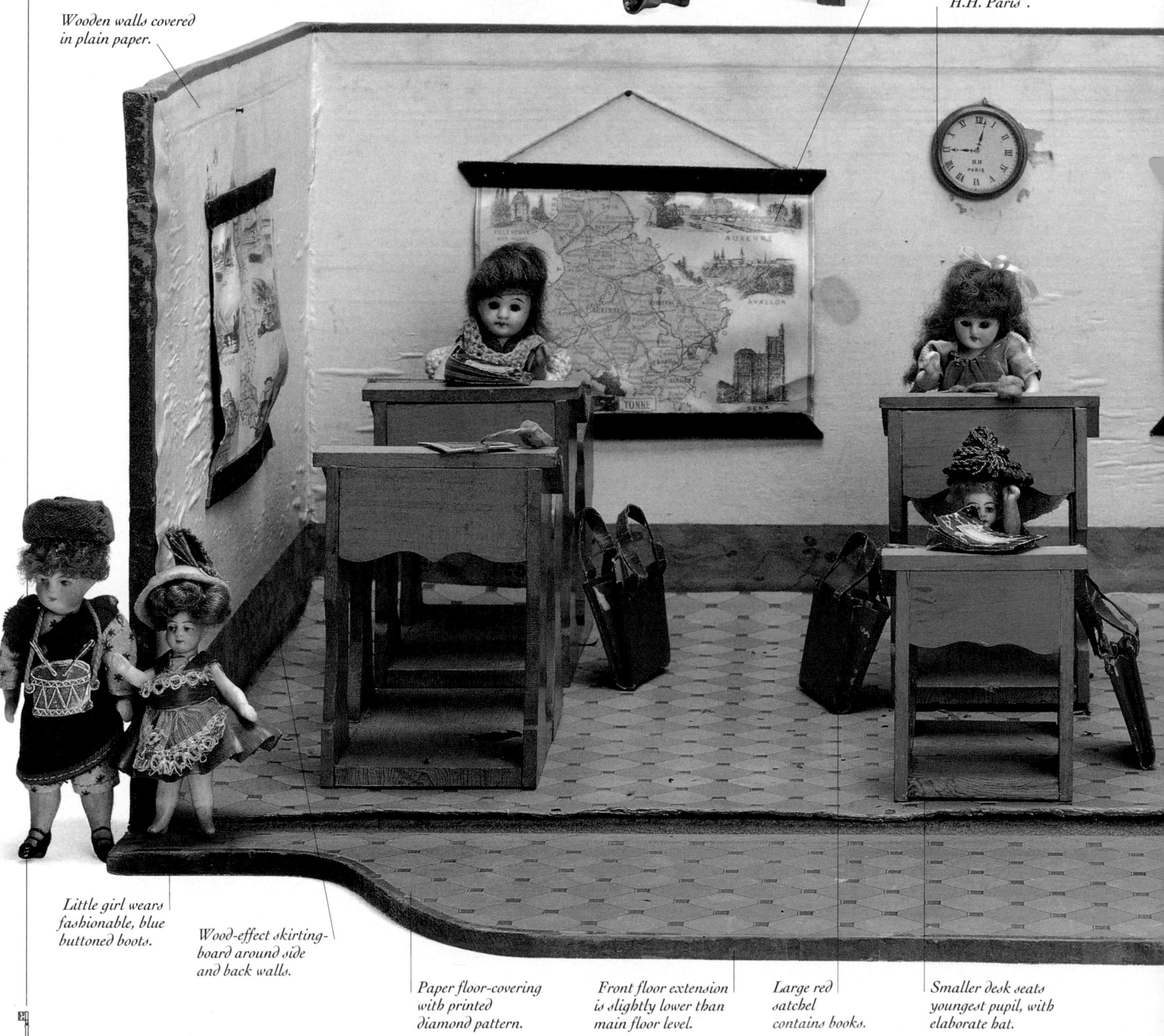

Illustrated wall-map of Yonne region of France.

Painted metal school clock in "brass" case is replacement. Metal face is marked "H.H. Paris".

Wooden walls covered in plain paper.

Little girl wears fashionable, blue buttoned boots.

Wood-effect skirting-board around side and back walls.

Paper floor-covering with printed diamond pattern.

Front floor extension is slightly lower than main floor level.

Large red satchel contains books.

Smaller desk seats youngest pupil, with elaborate hat.

FRENCH SCHOOLROOM

French, with additional German pieces; c.*1880–1900*

Jointed bisque doll with glass eyes and mohair wig.

MANY VERSIONS of the ever-popular toy schoolroom were produced in a three-sided box form. Often, if the room had a fourth wall, it was hinged to fold down flat at the front, forming part of the floor. This example, which has pale blue walls and a diamond tile-effect floor-paper, is a little unusual as the fourth wall is shaped, suggesting an apron-stage, which adds greatly to the charm of the setting.

Although the room and its furniture, including the six wooden desks and the blackboard, are French, many of the other contents, such as the pupils' large red satchels and writing-slates, with tiny pieces of sponge attached by string, are from Germany.

All the pupils are jointed bisque dolls with glass eyes and mohair wigs. None of them is wearing the traditional French schoolchild's black overall, so their clothes are more easily seen and admired. They are well dressed in a wide variety of outfits, from the red pleated dress and lace apron of the small doll standing on the left of the schoolroom, to the navy-blue outfits with sailor collars, worn by two dolls on the right. Three types of nineteenth-century children's footwear are displayed: shoes with ankle straps, shoes with two straps, and buttoned boots.

THE SCHOOLROOM

One of the most striking features in the schoolroom, apart from the pupils, is the set of wall-maps depicting four French regions: L'Ille-et-Vilaine, Basses Alpes, Yonne, and Drôme. The surrounding sketches of local historical buildings add greatly to the geographical detail.

Blackboard rests on simple wooden easel.

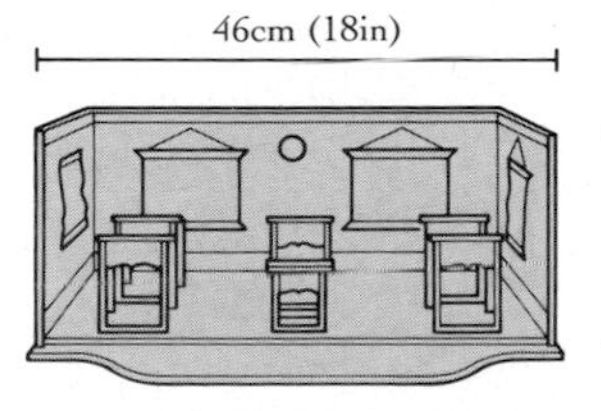

Box-shaped room with three walls and front flap.

Pupil wears navy-blue sailor-suit with white collar.

Metal school bell with wooden handle and metal clapper.

WASHINGTON DOLLS' HOUSE & TOY MUSEUM

FRENCH PARLOUR

French manufacturer; c.1880

ROOM SETTINGS, which have always been more popular in Europe than in Britain, where dolls' houses were preferred, were produced mainly in France and Germany. During their hey-day in the nineteenth century they were designed in a variety of styles, from the simple box shape to elaborately decorated two-room sets with an interconnecting door or archway.

This parlour is a fascinating example of *c.*1880 French elegance and charm; it also shows French ingenuity, for the whole room, when cleared of furniture, folds into a box whose base and front wall double as the "carpeted" floor when open.

The room's sumptuous appearance owes much to the rich, gilt-patterned wallpaper, above a dado of red flocked wallpaper, and the elegant curtains. Although most room sets were sold complete with furniture, the owner could add dolls and various accessories to enhance the appeal, as in this case.

TEA-SET *(BELOW)*
This enchanting little seven-piece porcelain tea-set, from the Sèvres works near Paris, is patterned with tiny roses and has a matching tray.

THE PARLOUR
All the ornaments, the books, and the newspaper, *Petit Journal pour Rire*, are later additions, but the furniture, pictures, and mirrors are original. The furniture includes an oval table, a sideboard, and five chairs upholstered in imitation leather. Both dolls are jointed bisques with glass eyes.

Gilt detail on oval tray.

Wooden walls fold into box; two angled windows.

Painted wooden container holds plant with delicate white flowers.

Front wall of box folds down to extend floor space.

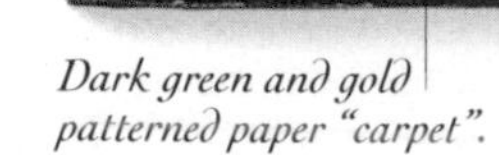

Dark green and gold patterned paper "carpet".

Chair, with narrow black paper strip imitating inlay, is one of set of five.

Decorative gold border.

Green wallpaper with gold star pattern above dado of crimson flocked paper.

Lace curtains adorn paper-framed window.

Striped green taffeta curtains with narrow gold braid trim.

Glass window set diagonally across one corner of room.

One of pair of hanging mirrors in gold paper frames.

Fragile fluted glass vase with gilded base.

Patterned wool rug with fringe on all sides, worked in cross-stitch.

Jointed bisque doll holds cup-and-ball toy.

Miniature book dated 1895, Les Rondes de l'Enfance, *with illustrated words and music.*

WASHINGTON DOLLS' HOUSE & TOY MUSEUM

TWO-ROOM SETTING

German; Rock & Graner furniture; c.*1880–1900*

WURTTEMBERG, IN SOUTH-WEST GERMANY, produced many notable toy-makers. Apart from the Schoenhut family *(see pp.92–93)*, one of the best known names today is Rock & Graner, a firm renowned for the pressed-tin-plate dolls' house furniture that it started making *c.*1850.

This two-room setting with its Rock & Graner furniture was bought in Zurich, Switzerland, at the turn of the century; it is completely furnished with metal items, mostly Rock & Graner's distinctive dark brown pieces, hand-painted to resemble wood-grain. These contrast well with the delicate pale wallpapers, light and bright curtains, and warm-toned floors, all of which were part of the original room setting.

THE INTERIOR
Although the curtains and floor- and wallpapers in this setting are original, many decorative items, including gilt picture frames, clocks, mirrors, and flower-filled *jardinières*, have been added.

Rock & Graner settee with silk-covered seat, from drawing-room set.

Gilt metal clip holds lace pelmet in place.

Closed wooden "louvred" shutters.

Window with open shutters and curtains.

Painted stone effect on wall.

Brass knob fixed to hinged shutter.

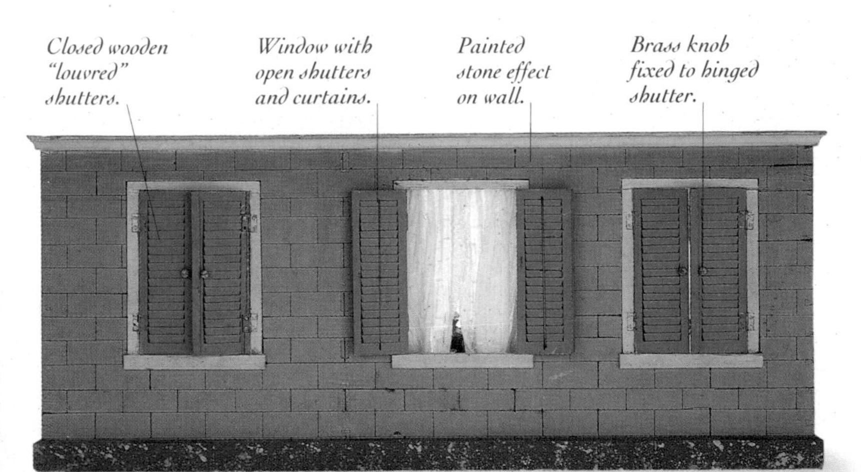

THE EXTERIOR

Each of the three glazed windows on the back wall is fitted with a pair of hinged, green-painted "louvred" shutters.

Metal flue runs from stove to wall.

STOVE *(RIGHT)*

This elegant stove with attached flue provides heating in the bedroom. It is finished in enamel with two gold bands.

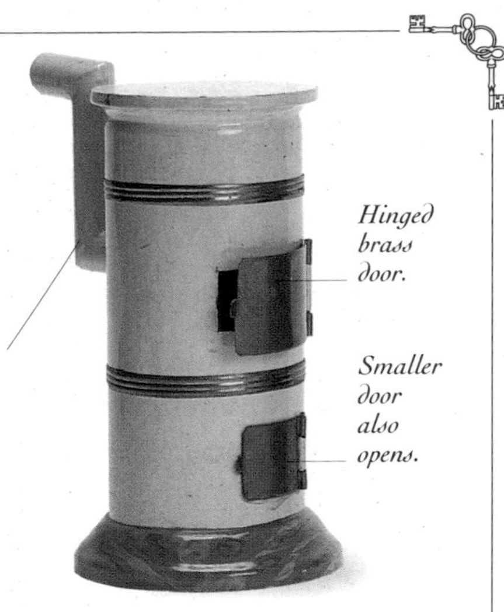

Hinged brass door.

Smaller door also opens.

Rock & Graner jardinière *filled with flowering plants.*

Hinged lid of wash-stand open, revealing toilet items inside.

Decorative pelmet of lace, braid, and beads.

Metal oil-lamp with milk-glass bowl and glass chimney.

Gilded metal light fitting.

Painted metal plaque is one of a pair.

Rock & Graner painted metal bed.

SIDEBOARD *(BELOW)*

The upper shelf of this Rock & Graner sideboard displays a clock and two pictures in gilt frames; the shelf is supported by two gilded sea-serpents.

Coiled beeswax candle.

Metal sideboard painted to resemble wood-grain.

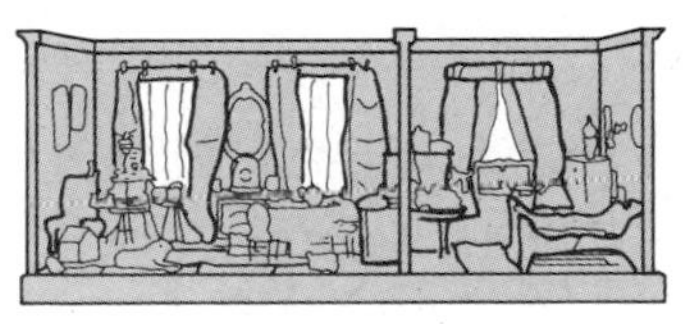

Two-room setting; three glazed windows with hinged shutters.

BUTCHER'S SHOP

German; made by Christian Hacker; c.1900

THIS BUTCHER'S SHOP, which was given to a young English girl *c.*1905, was made by the German toy-maker Christian Hacker, probably around the turn of the century. Based in Nuremberg, the firm began producing dolls' houses and shops in the mid-1870s. Christian Hacker also made dolls' house furniture, another popular line, and toy kitchens; like the shops, these were regarded as educational aids in teaching young girls household management skills, hence the degree of realism in the modelling and painting of the joints of meat.

As the shop was a plaything as well as a teaching toy, it is surprising that it has remained so well stocked with wares and equipment. The survival of the realistically modelled butcher in his traditional costume is particularly fortunate.

Removable pediment held in place by pins.

Original wallpaper suggests tiles.

Unjointed carcass hangs on hook.

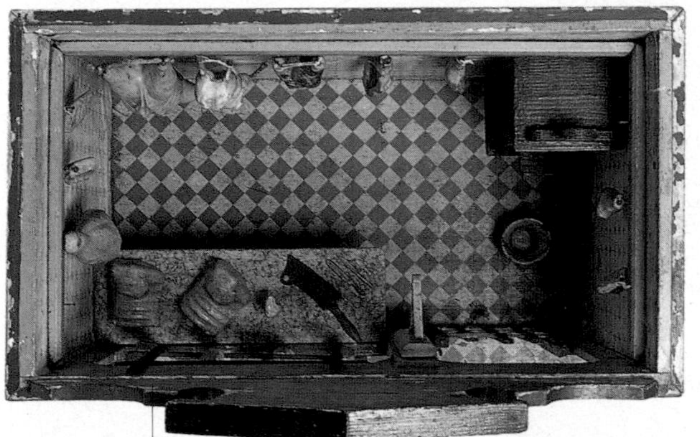

OVERHEAD VIEW The fixed counter provides a display area for meat as well as a cutting surface; a meat cleaver and selection of knives are visible here, as is the original diamond-patterned floor-paper. The cash-booth is movable.

Shop has open top behind fascia.

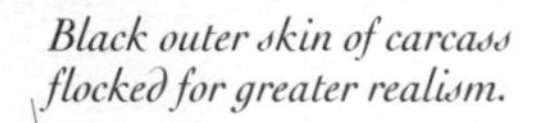

Black outer skin of carcass flocked for greater realism.

Joints hang from rack in window.

BUTCHER'S MEAT *(RIGHT)* All types of meat are sold here, including wild boar. The joints are cut in the continental way, providing a clue to the origins of the shop and its contents.

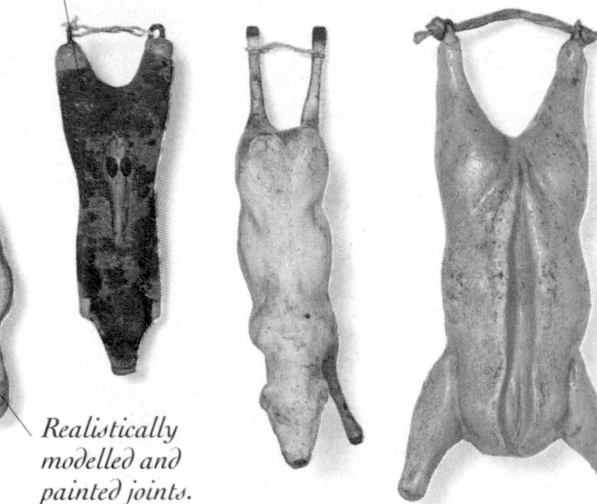

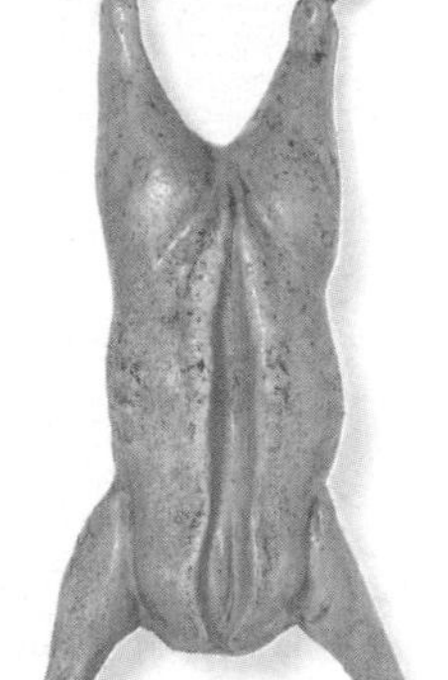

Realistically modelled and painted joints.

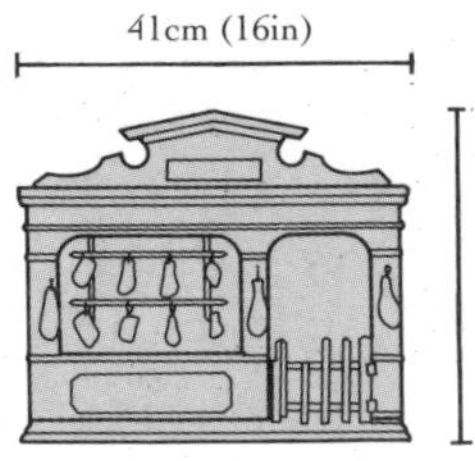

Open box design; hinged gate and cash-booth door.

Characteristic Christian Hacker paintwork in cream, red, and black.

Ornate gilded panels typical of Christian Hacker houses and room sets.

English words suggest shop was made for export.

Facade is decorated with gilded frieze.

Butcher wears German-style clothes including smock, baggy trousers, gaiters, and cap.

Wooden lattice gate across shop entrance has metal handle and hinges.

THE FACADE AND INTERIOR

Only a glimpse of the shop interior can be seen from the outside. The original contents, and the diamond-patterned paper on the floor and walls, have not suffered as much damage as the typical Hacker paintwork and decorated panels on the facade.

One of several metal knives.

Wooden-handled meat cleaver.

Painted metal bucket.

BUTCHER'S EQUIPMENT

(ABOVE) The metal meat cleaver was designed to hang from a nail, while the painted metal bucket was provided to stand under uncut hanging carcasses.

Metal hinge on cash-booth door.

CASH-BOOTH *(ABOVE)*

The wooden cash-booth has a hinged front, giving access to the seat behind the window-counter. It has a carved fascia board, and a paper "Cash" sign above the window opening.

TIN BATHROOM

German; c.1920s

UNLIKE A FULLY FITTED TOY KITCHEN, which fascinates by its wealth of everyday items, the bathroom has few contents and little decoration. Yet it has proved a popular toy for generations of children, especially when, as in this example, water is available "on tap". This apparently simple little painted metal room set hides a complex system of working taps and drains. The pump draws water into tanks on the back walls, and from these the bath and basin are filled, the lavatory is flushed, and the shower supplied.

This example is relatively well appointed, with a gilded mirror, toilet-roll-holder, towel-rails, fluffy towels, and a matching bath-mat; there is even a bathroom thermometer.

Any fears that too many cold baths might have removed the doll's colouring and frozen her stiff are ill-founded; little figures such as this were always made of glazed white ceramic.

Round, gilt-framed mirror suspended from hook on side wall.
Metal tap swivels to control water supply.
Metal comb on hand-basin.

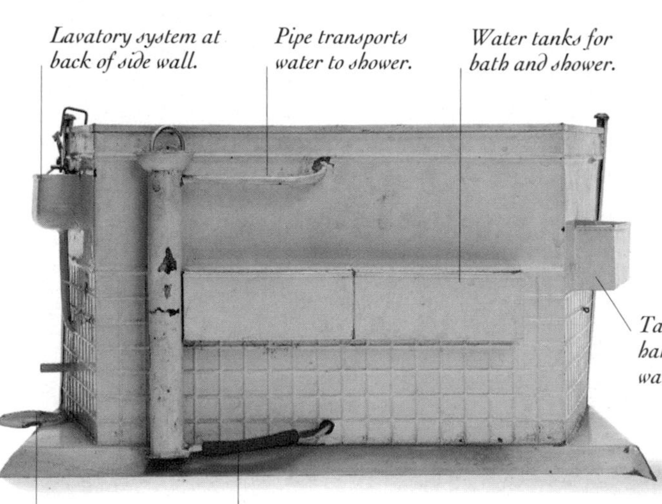
Lavatory system at back of side wall.
Pipe transports water to shower.
Water tanks for bath and shower.
Tank holds hand-basin's water supply.
Ledge originally held waste-water container.
Rubber tube connects bath's drainage pipe to pump.

PLUMBING SYSTEM *(ABOVE)*
Having turned on the appropriate tap, water from a tank on the back wall is pumped into the bath or shower-head by pulling the ring on top of the pump up and down. Waste is then returned from the bath to the system via a waste pipe.

33cm (13in)

19cm (7½in)

Painted tin bathroom; "plumbed-in" water supply.

THE BATHROOM
The lower walls in this simple tin bathroom have a stamped tile pattern, while the upper walls are painted blue with gilt picture rail and dado rail. The bath, the lavatory, and the basin are tin. The taps, towel-rails, and shower-head are brass.

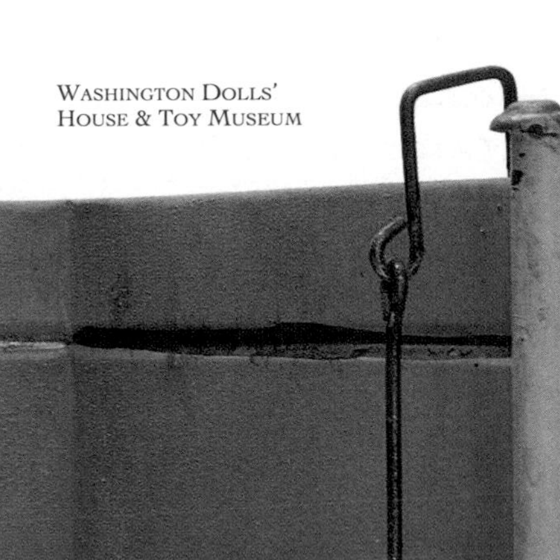

LAVATORY CISTERN *(LEFT)*
The lavatory has a cistern behind the right side wall, the "flush" being operated by a system of levers from the cistern to a ring that once hung beside the lavatory. A container originally stood on the ledge under the cistern to collect waste water.

WASHINGTON DOLLS' HOUSE & TOY MUSEUM

Commercially Made Dolls' Houses

During the nineteenth century, the concept of miniature houses changed as they began to be commercially produced in quantity, and the ornamental "baby houses" of adult collectors evolved into "dolls' houses" intended as childrens' playthings. In the mid-twentieth century another phase began: adults as well as children began to enjoy the charms of modern dolls' houses, and antique playthings were increasingly sought by collectors.

RESEARCH BY VIVIEN GREENE, the English authority on dolls' houses, has revealed that the famous London toy-seller Bellamy advertised a list of "toys" for adults and children in his December 1762 trade-card: "Baby-houses, with all Sorts of Furniture at the lowest Price. Wholesale and Retail." This suggests that some commercially produced dolls' houses were made for children in England earlier than is usually supposed. From the middle of the nineteenth century, however, dolls' houses as playthings were certainly being manufactured in large quantities, mainly by German and English firms.

As Dickens vividly illustrates in his portrayal of Caleb, the toy-maker in *The Cricket on the Hearth*, most English dolls' houses in the mid-nineteenth century were produced at home by craftsmen who sold their houses wholesale to shops. If Caleb is a typical example (and Dickens is generally regarded as a reliable reporter), these craftsmen produced a prodigious variety of houses: "... suburban tenements for dolls of moderate means; kitchens and single apartments for dolls of the lowest classes; capital town residences for dolls of high estate ... some already furnished according to estimate ... others could be filled at a moment's notice, from whole shelves of chairs and tables, sofas, bedsteads, and upholstery".

FRENCH SEASIDE VILLAS *(LEFT)*
Mon Repos (far left and pp.80–81) *is a very decorative dolls' house with two lavishly wall-papered rooms. The house next to it is a later, plainer, and obviously cheaper version. It, too, has steps to a porticoed front door, a door to a balcony, and a mock attic window, but its interior walls are not wallpapered.*

1914 ENGLISH COTTAGE
(ABOVE) This unusual papier-mâché and wood cottage was commercially made, according to its label, by Mrs Florence Callcott. It is open-backed, with a hinged painted door and windows, and internal staircase.

DOLLY'S PLAY HOUSE
(RIGHT) McLoughlin Brothers of New York produced this lavishly decorated, printed paper-covered folding dolls' house from c.1884 to 1903 in brighter colours than those suggested by the box-lid.

Well into the twentieth century, many British dolls' house manufacturers and retailers were based in London, as were the warehouses of imported dolls' houses, which came mainly from Germany. London children were well served: Silber & Fleming (manufacturers and importers) and Cremer (importer and toy shop); the stalls in the Lawther Arcade and Morrell's famous shop in the Burlington Arcade; Gamages and Whiteleys department stores – these are just some of the names that make today's dolls' house collectors long for the loan of a time machine.

During the nineteenth century, English and German dolls' houses were being exported to the United States where they were advertised in the catalogues of stores such as F.A.O. Schwarz and Sears Roebuck, along with best-selling lines from American manufacturers like Bliss, Schoenhut, McLoughlin, and Converse. Dolls' houses never achieved as much popularity in the Mediterranean countries as they did in the northern regions. Museums in Denmark, Norway, and Sweden contain several interesting nineteenth-century dolls' houses; some of these were imported from Germany, but others were made, and at least partially furnished, in Scandinavia. Several of the most famous modern dolls' house and miniature furniture manufacturers are Scandinavian: products of the Swedish firm Lundby are distributed throughout the world, and pieces by Brio (also Swedish) and the Danish firm Hanse, which reflect current fashions and styles, attract adults as well as children.

— FAMOUS NAMES —

For nearly two centuries, however, it was the German and British manufacturers, joined later by American firms, who produced most of the dolls' houses, furniture, and accessories that are

BLISS FURNITURE *(RIGHT)*
From c.1888 until 1901 R. Bliss of Pawtucket, Rhode Island, advertised dolls' house furniture packed "in strong pasteboard boxes" with "beautifully lithographed labels". This set of lithographed parlour furniture contains a piano, table, sofa, and chairs. Bliss made other similar sets, including one of bedroom furniture.

SILBER & FLEMING DOLLS' HOUSE *(BELOW) The dolls' houses produced by this c.1850–1900 London manufacturer and importer ranged from small two-room villas to six-room mansions with staircases. Most were "box backs" with front-opening facades and painted stone and brickwork. Countless Victorian nurseries possessed a variation of this typical best-selling design.*

now the much-prized possessions of contemporary collectors. Dolls' houses made by Moritz Gottschalk (1865–1939) and Christian Hacker (1870–1914); pressed-tin furniture, painted to resemble wood, by Rock & Graner (1825–1904); "Waltershausen" imitation inlaid rosewood pieces by Schneegas (1830s–1940); and filigree metal furniture made by Schweitzer (founded in 1796 and still in production) are all held in high regard and command correspondingly high prices. The same may be said about the tin-plate furniture made by the English firm Evans & Cartwright (1800–80) and the gilded metal pieces, which often included "novelty" needlecases in the shape of miniature chairs, by Avery & Sons (*c.*1860s).

Even twentieth-century dolls' houses, such as those made by Lines (1919–71), and furnished by Elgin (1919–26) or Barton (1945–84), are seen by some as collectors' items in the 1990s.

— HOUSING PREFERENCES —

The English have traditionally chosen houses rather than room sets, attracted by their realistic facades. To a large extent, dolls' houses have been favoured in the United States also. In Europe, however, and especially in France and Germany, room settings have usually been preferred.

Most nineteenth-century dolls' houses in the middle or upper price range were made of wood, painted to resemble brick and stone, but some excellent paper and cardboard models were also produced; these became particularly popular in

1928 CARDBOARD HOUSES *(LEFT)*
Cheap cardboard dolls' houses were popular in the United States during the 1920s. Sears Roebuck's 1928 catalogue offered a six-room house, and a bungalow in two sizes.

the United States toward the end of the nineteenth century. By 1910, various American manufacturers were producing very well-printed designs; probably the most famous name was that of McLoughlin Brothers *(see pp.86–87)*, whose lines of printed, folding houses were also exported to the United Kingdom.

Before the introduction of plastic, tin or a heavier sheet metal was used for dolls' houses, room settings, and furniture. In the United States, as early as 1869, Louis Marx, Mettoy, and several lesser known firms were producing attractive, brightly lithographed tin-plate buildings. Today, plastic materials are used extensively by modern manufacturers. Two current best-sellers are the Playmobil *c.*1900-style mansion, which is made entirely from brightly coloured, injection-moulded plastic, and the open-fronted houses, made by the Swedish firm Lundby, which are constructed from a mixture of plastic, fibreboard, and wood.

Houses supplied in kit form are also popular. A British firm, Hobbies of Dereham, has provided such plans and materials for decades *(see pp.94–95)*. Books of printed paper and cardboard houses, which have only to be cut out, and stuck or slotted together, also sell well. Several have been made with printed interior rooms, and some have furniture printed on the walls. One ingenious version, described as a "carousel pop-up book house", is illustrated on page 112.

But even in these plastic-dominated days, painted wood is still the favourite material for Caleb's successors who make the dolls' houses that are now sold in specialist shops, and are designed for children or adults to furnish – if not at "the lowest prices" as advertised by Bellamy in 1762, still "with all Sorts of Furniture".

SCHOENHUT ROOM *(LEFT)*
This room is from a house made by Schoenhut of Philadelphia. The walls are simply painted with stencilled friezes and cut-out doorways. Its dolls and furniture are recent additions.

TWINKY DOLLS *(ABOVE)*
In 1964 the American firm Grandmother Stover advertised these jointed, plastic dolls' house dolls, all painted and dressed by Ethel Strong, who commissioned the dolls from a moulder.

No. 12

Possibly English or German; c.1870s

BOX-BACK DOLLS' HOUSES, like the one featured here, were to be found in many late-nineteenth-century nurseries, as such dolls' houses were being commercially produced at that time. But because this house has no maker's mark or distinguishing feature, and because so many models like it were being made in England and Germany at this period, it is difficult to be sure of the house's exact origins.

Although the exterior of No. 12 is plain, apart from its balconies and decorative brickwork, the interior displays genuine 1870s patterned wallpapers, carpets, and furnishings (mostly German), a plethora of pictures and ornaments, and an "Upstairs, Downstairs" household of 11 doll inhabitants. "No. 12", incidentally, was discovered painted on the front door of the house.

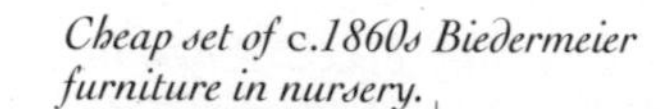

Cheap set of c.1860s Biedermeier furniture in nursery.

Original metal fireplace in nursery.

Wooden kitchen dresser fixed to side wall.

Kitchen table has long drawer and hinged side extensions.

Painted wooden quoining.

Decorative "brick" lintels painted over window.

Ornate metal balcony, painted maroon and gold.

Balusters nailed to wooden floor and top-rail.

Cream-painted window-ledge.

Steps nailed to fixed front door.

Painted wooden door.

THE FACADE
The metal balconies and "brick" lintels above the windows redeem somewhat the facade of this simple box-back house, which has no other features on the back or sides. Each of the 14 glazed windows has one painted glazing bar, and a small wooden window-ledge.

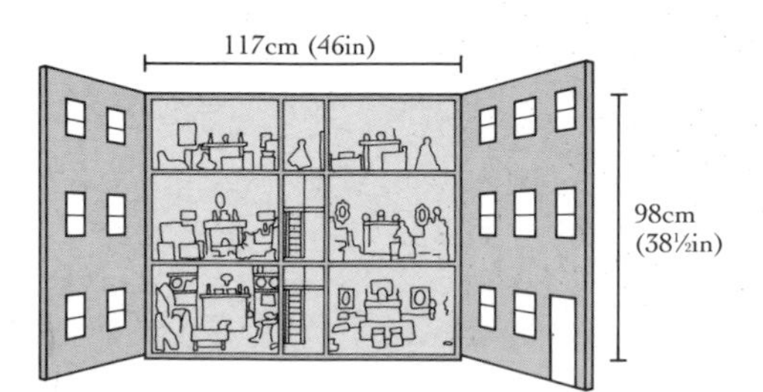

Box-back house; hinged two-section front opening.

Very thick, shiny, embossed and gilded paper.

Chimney-breast extends through all floors.

Blocked-in fireplace below mantelpiece in maids' room.

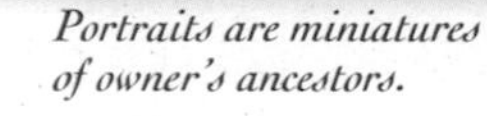

Second Floor
A brass fender guards the fire in the nursery *(left)*, where a child is playing. The room is furnished with simple wooden furniture, as is the maids' room *(right)*, which also contains a plain, tin hip-bath.

China basin and ewer on wooden wash-stand.

First Floor
The drawing-room *(right)* and bedroom *(left)* are furnished in Victorian style with a wealth of pictures, mirrors, ornaments, and lamps, as well as Waltershausen furniture. Next to the bed is a set of bed-steps and a chamber-pot.

Candle sconces and chandeliers provide lighting.

Oriental, carved ivory elephant candle-holder.

Chandelier raised and lowered by pulley and chain.

Gilt-framed prints on side walls.

Ground Floor
Adjacent to the hall are the kitchen *(left)*, with its original black metal kitchen range, and the dining-room *(right)*, which is fashionably decorated in crimson and gilt, and furnished with a set of Waltershausen furniture, a "marble" fireplace, and gilt-framed portraits.

Removable stairs with high risers.

1870s painted wallpaper provides "tiles" in hall.

Dining-room carpet made from part of wool Paisley shawl.

Portraits are miniatures of owner's ancestors.

Flocked panels on dado.

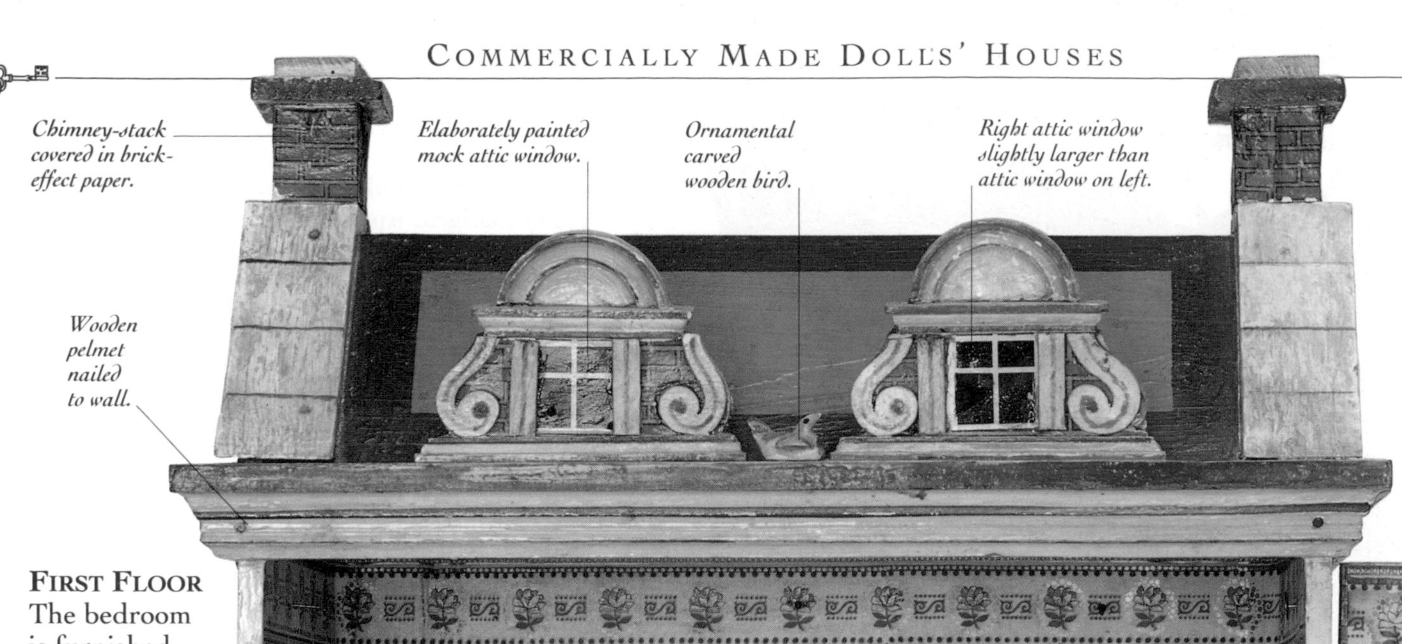

Chimney-stack covered in brick-effect paper.

Elaborately painted mock attic window.

Ornamental carved wooden bird.

Right attic window slightly larger than attic window on left.

Elaborately patterned wallpaper in excellent condition.

Wooden pelmet nailed to wall.

FIRST FLOOR
The bedroom is furnished with printed, paper-covered furniture and a filigree-framed mirror. A dado is pasted over the basic wallpapers.

Scrap-covered folding screen complements lithographed furniture.

Floral arrangement made of painted, moulded lead.

Delicate filigree metal picture-frame.

GROUND FLOOR
The sitting-room is furnished with a very pretty set of lithographed chairs and settee, and a German-made filigree metal fireplace.

Painted bark covers front and sides of base, suggesting rock.

All-bisque child doll seated at wooden piano.

MON REPOS

Probably German; c.1890s–1900s

THE STYLE OF THIS DELIGHTFUL small house has been described as resembling that of a late-nineteenth-century French seaside villa. The facade suggests a more spacious interior than the house actually possesses: there are just two rooms, without even a staircase between them. The interior splendour is confined to the unexpectedly elaborate wallpapers – red and green versions of the same pattern. Both rooms have wooden pelmets, draped curtains, and the same detailed, patterned, printed paper floor-covering; the inner surfaces of the doors are surprisingly crude. The windows are very attractive: those in the attic are ornately painted, and the glazed lower ones are fitted with venetian blinds. Bark, representing rock, has been nailed to the deep base.

Backing of venetian blinds behind curtains.

Lace-edged curtains looped back with metal hooks.

Brick-effect paper from facade folded around edge.

Inner surface of door crudely finished.

Lace-trimmed cotton curtains at glazed bay window.

Door hinged to open inwards.

Unusual orange-painted roof with brown border.

Green paper venetian blinds pasted inside windows.

Door opens onto balcony with balustrade.

Roof of bay window painted in similar style to main roof.

Steep flight of painted wooden steps.

THE FACADE
Although German dolls' house manufacturers were influenced by contemporary styles of architecture, they did not confine themselves to making only miniature replicas. Mon Repos bears no manufacturer's mark, but it is probably one of the many German dolls' houses that were designed to appeal to a specific export market.

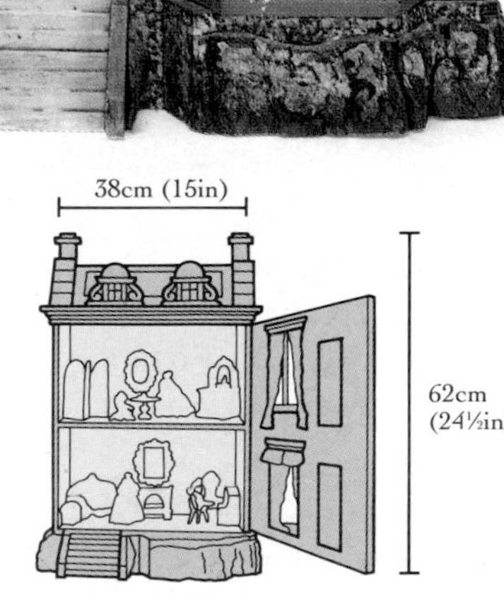

Painted and papered wood; hinged front opening.

HACKER HOUSE

Made in Germany; c.1890s

THE NUREMBERG FIRM Christian Hacker was founded in the 1870s but this dolls' house was probably made nearer the turn of the century. It is an unusual version of a design that was usually constructed with only two floors. The different decoration of the third floor, which is the only one with side bay windows, suggests that this may have been a later addition – a relatively easy alteration, as the roof was designed to be removable. However, the manufacturer did produce many variations of certain basic designs.

Some original floor-papers remain and the wallpaper in all five rooms is old, although it was added after the house was purchased. There are interior doors, but no staircase; the windows are glazed and the front doors are hinged to open.

House is of simple "box on box" construction.

Three-paned bay window on side wall of top floor.

Printed paper decoration below and above top window.

Decorative transfer on panel.

Door originally opened onto balcony.

Cotton blind inside window.

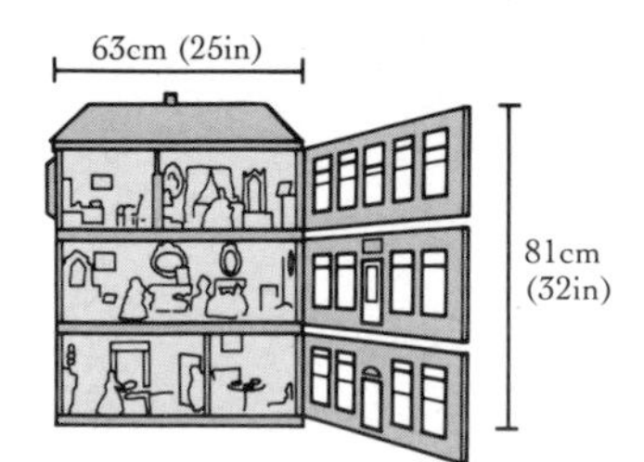

Wooden structure; three hinged facade sections.

THE FACADE
Each of the floors of this house has a separate hinged facade section. Ornamental panels on the first two floors are transfers, but the third-floor section has printed paper decorations. The door on the first floor indicates that the house once had a balcony.

Rock & Graner tinplate chaise longue covered in silk.

Dado of dark wood-grain-effect paper.

Typical Christian Hacker line decoration.

Dresser lacks original base section.

Painted wooden roof, with small central chimney, lifts off.

Hinges for top-floor opening facade smaller than those on other two floors, suggesting this is addition.

Decorative gold braid pelmet surmounts lace curtains.

Photograph of Queen Alexandra, wife of British monarch Edward VII, in decorative metal frame.

Cane cradle lacks original rockers.

SECOND FLOOR

Both rooms on this floor are arranged as bedrooms, with a connecting door. In each room is a side bay window draped with white lace curtains and gold braid pelmet. Although most of the furniture is Waltershausen, the most interesting item is the Rock & Graner half-tester bed in the smaller room on the left. Equally charming, but less rare, are the pink and black painted tin bath set and the cane cradle in the larger bedroom *(right)*.

Child's portrait in gilded pressed-metal frame.

Larger hinges used on front opening sections of lower floors.

Fashionably attired doll wears blue dress with train.

Side panels and front of sideboard richly decorated.

FIRST FLOOR

The drawing-room occupies the whole of this floor; it has no side windows, doors, or access to other floors. The room is handsomely furnished with a lavishly decorated suite of chromolithographed pieces and a Rock & Graner chaise longue upholstered in purple silk. On the chaise longue is a miniature copy of *Weldon's Ladies' Journal.*

Typically dark but lavishly patterned late-nineteenth-century wallpaper.

Painted bronze roses in flowerpot.

Pressed-tin arm-chair upholstered in red velvet.

Original geometrically patterned floor-paper.

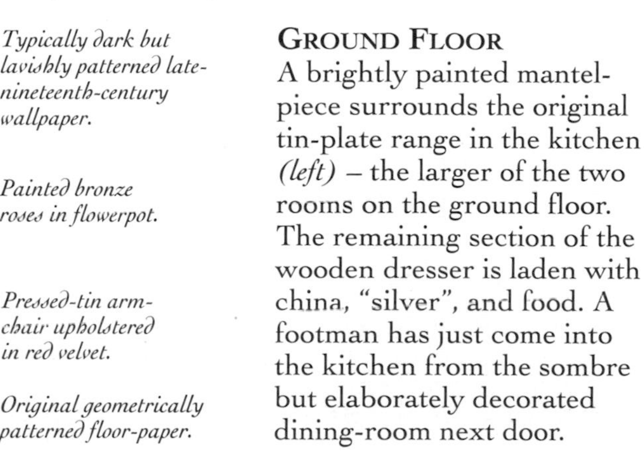

GROUND FLOOR

A brightly painted mantelpiece surrounds the original tin-plate range in the kitchen *(left)* – the larger of the two rooms on the ground floor. The remaining section of the wooden dresser is laden with china, "silver", and food. A footman has just come into the kitchen from the sombre but elaborately decorated dining-room next door.

GERMAN FURNISHINGS

THE CHRISTIAN HACKER HOUSE contains many excellent examples of different types of mid- to late-nineteenth-century dolls' house furniture; the chromolithographed pieces in the drawing-room are particularly eye-catching, while the Rock & Graner chaise longue, pedestal table, and small half-tester bed, draped with green curtains, are of great interest to collectors. Other unusual items include the pressed-tin armchair, which is upholstered in red velvet. The work of Waltershausen toy-makers is well represented, the piano in the drawing-room being noteworthy.

Elegant wooden chair covered in chromolithographed paper.

Chair upholstered in pink velvet, edged with gilt paper braid.

Sideboard covered in decorated paper panels.

Cupid design popular in 1880s.

Door of sideboard hinged to open.

Hinged, slightly curved door.

DECORATIVE FURNITURE *(ABOVE)* The chair and pair of sideboards are excellent examples of plain wooden items that have been transformed by the application of chromolithographed paper.

Fireplace has painted coal, alight and smoking.

FIREPLACE *(LEFT)* The gilded, pierced metal ornamentation, enhanced by a black fire-back with painted fire effect, made this tiny fireplace a best seller.

DRESSER *(BELOW)* It is likely that this is only the top section of the dresser and that the base is now missing. The contents of the shelves were probably all made in Thuringia – but the portrait is of the British monarch Edward VII.

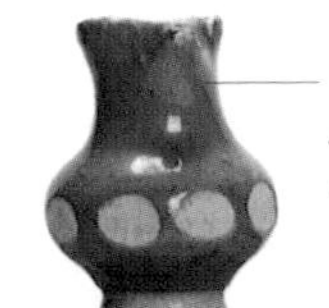

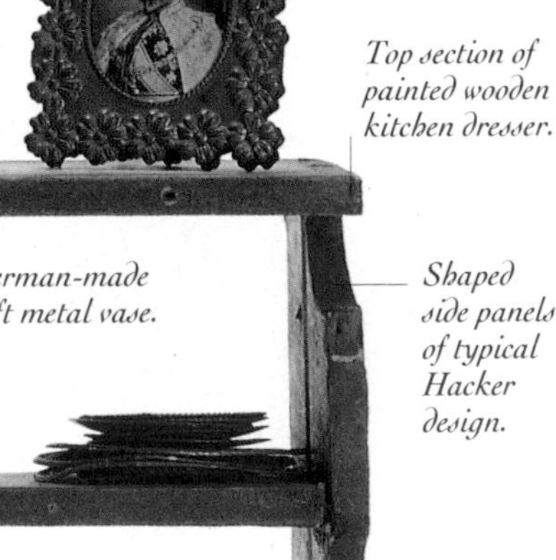

Cream and brown pottery jug.

Wooden bowl made in Germany.

Typical design for small, mass-produced jugs.

Photograph in ornate metal frame.

Top section of painted wooden kitchen dresser.

Painted plaster orange on wooden plate.

Painted, moulded plaster sandwiches on plate.

Stack of painted wooden plates.

German-made soft metal vase.

Shaped side panels of typical Hacker design.

Pierced tin tray with matching glass holders.

WALTERSHAUSEN FURNITURE *(BELOW)*
Waltershausen, in Thuringia, was a centre of wooden toy-making. The bureau and chest of drawers were made by Schneegas, a local firm renowned for its imitation rosewood and gilt furniture.

Painted bronze rose in pot.

Simulated rosewood bureau decorated with gilt transfers.

Silk-covered seat of chair edged with gilt paper braid.

Drawers ornamented with "Gothic" transfers.

China toilet set decorated with "onion pattern" design.

Chest of drawers with marble top, used as wash-stand.

Piano has reversed key colouring.

Decorative pink panel of upright piano edged with gilt paper.

NINETEENTH-CENTURY GERMAN LADIES

FIVE GERMAN DOLLS' HOUSE DOLLS are shown in the Christian Hacker house, but the china-headed doll with the fashionable hat may be a visitor. Although it is likely that the dolls were all dressed after purchase, the costumes of the two from the drawing room *(left and right, below)* have been elaborately trimmed and pleated with considerable skill. The identical bisque-headed dolls have finely moulded hairstyles; the footman and visitor are china-headed dolls with black hair. All the dolls have soft stitch-jointed bodies with bisque lower arms and legs, a type that was popular from *c.*1870 until 1890.

Elaborately moulded bisque hairstyle.

Doll has bisque head and limbs, and soft body.

Dress based on mid-1870s English style.

Extensively pleated home-made dress.

Identical twin of other bisque-headed example (left).

Plain tailored outfit with velvet trimming.

China-headed doll with shiny black-painted hair.

Fashionable hat fixed to doll's head.

Checked and embroidered dress with elaborately pleated train.

THE PRETTY VILLAGE

American; produced by McLoughlin Brothers, New York in 1897

BEST KNOWN FOR the fine colour printing of their larger and heavier cardboard dolls' houses, all with sumptuously decorated interiors, McLoughlin Brothers first produced "The Pretty Village" in 1897. It proved to be extremely popular and several different editions were printed over a number of years. All editions were sold in large boxes with attractive and colourful pictures on the lids *(see p.73)*.

Constructing the village was simple: you had to cut out a building, fold and glue the tabs in place, then either position the finished product on the planned base, for which directions were given, or design a village layout to your own specifications.

Although these buildings are small and printed only on the exterior, children derived hours of pleasure from making them up and then planning the layout. The village shown here has eight houses, and includes a log cabin, a school, a fire-station, a blacksmith's shop, a boat-house, and a photographer's studio. Sadly, it has none of the free-standing cut-out figures found in some sets.

COTTAGE *(ABOVE)*
The child in this cottage, with its red-tiled roof, is happy and industrious like all the children in The Pretty Village.

9cm (3½in)

9cm (3½in)

No access to interior; details printed in full colour on card.

Child fishes alongside "Friendship Boat Club" boat-house.

BOAT-HOUSE *(BELOW)*
The layout plan of this building includes a waterfront.

GREENHOUSE *(BELOW)*
This charming greenhouse, well-stocked with colourful and tropical plants, belongs to M.A. Flower the Florist.

CLAPBOARD HOUSE *(BELOW)* This pretty clapboard house has a shingled gable, two balconies, and a veranda.

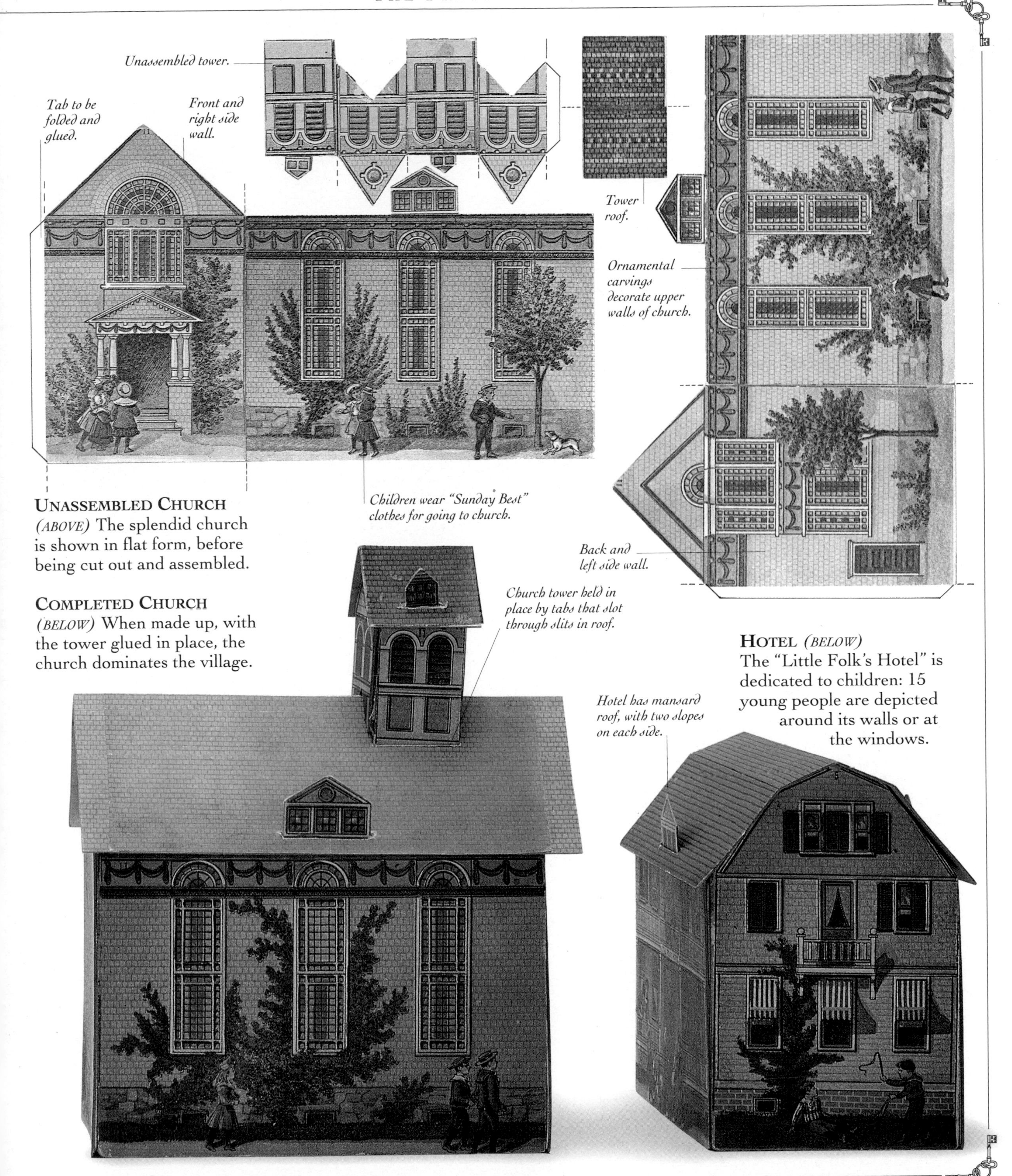

UNASSEMBLED CHURCH *(ABOVE)* The splendid church is shown in flat form, before being cut out and assembled.

COMPLETED CHURCH *(BELOW)* When made up, with the tower glued in place, the church dominates the village.

HOTEL *(BELOW)* The "Little Folk's Hotel" is dedicated to children: 15 young people are depicted around its walls or at the windows.

Canoe and Dog *(above)*
The canoe is made of birch bark stitched to framework. The hunting hound has a well-moulded, skin-covered body with painted features.

First Floor
Only one upstairs room is visible at the back, but there is a side attic with an open window, accessible when the hinged roof is lifted up.

Ground Floor
Both the main room and the kitchen have hinged doors and open windows. The plainly furnished rooms have decorative rugs on the floor.

Tripod and Pot *(below)*
Rolled birch-bark shavings provide the "logs" for this camp-fire. A cooking-pot hangs from the tripod; both are made of blackwood.

ADIRONDACK COTTAGE

American; probably made by Bliss of Pawtucket in 1904

THE NATIONAL NOVELTY CORPORATION was selling the "Adirondack Cottage novel dolls' house" in 1904, but no mention was made in their advertisements of the manufacturer's name. However, given the quality of construction and the materials used (lithographed paper-covered wood) and Bliss's later references to its production of "cabins", the most likely contender seems to be Bliss of Pawtucket, Rhode Island – at that time a member of the National Novelty Corporation.

The exterior walls are covered in lithographed log-patterned paper, the interior walls with a wood finish, while the base has a chequered blackwood top with stones and mortar sides. The lithographed stags' heads on the gables are purely decorative, but the American Indian figurehead on the side attic roof acts as a handle. Although the window openings are unglazed, two lithographed windows on the right side wall suggest glazing, with green blinds downstairs and frilly curtains upstairs. The doors are plain, but the balcony and gable have decorative features. The design that was originally advertised had more ornamental features, including a papered stone-effect chimney.

Carved wooden handle with lithographed American Indian figurehead.

Bamboo table with clay bowl.

Original position of lithographed chimney, now missing.

Steeply pitched roof designed to withstand heavy snow.

Lithographed design identical on both sides of handle.

Flannel rug printed with American Indian design.

Hinged door with metal catch.

THE FACADE
This lithographed structure represents the style of log-cabin found in the Adirondacks, a mountainous area in New York State. Some of the house's decorative features reflect American Indian culture.

WASHINGTON DOLLS' HOUSE & TOY MUSEUM

44cm (17½in)

44cm (17½in)

Wooden structure; open-backed; two hinged doors.

BLISS HOUSE

American; made by Bliss of Pawtucket; c.*1904*

RUFUS BLISS ESTABLISHED the Bliss Manufacturing Company in 1832 to make wooden piano screws. He retired in 1863, but the firm later started manufacturing toys. Between *c.*1890 and 1914, it produced the dolls' houses that made the Bliss name famous. From 1903 until 1907 Bliss and other leading American toy-makers traded together as the National Novelty Corporation; during these years many Bliss houses were sold by the Corporation. Bliss lines continued in production despite a later take-over, and this particular design was still selling in 1920, confirming not only its popularity but also the firm's reputation for well-made products, a point that Bliss had always emphasized when advertising.

In addition to dolls' houses (designs ranged from log-cabins to suburban residences), Bliss also produced stables, shops, warehouses, and even fire-stations and a fort. All these toys, like the dolls' houses, were constructed of wood covered with colourful lithographed paper.

FIRST FLOOR

Despite its elaborate facade, the house has a simple interior with only one main room on each floor, and no staircase. The out-of-scale wallpaper marks this house as a later Bliss model, and contrasts vividly with the well-proportioned lithographed exterior.

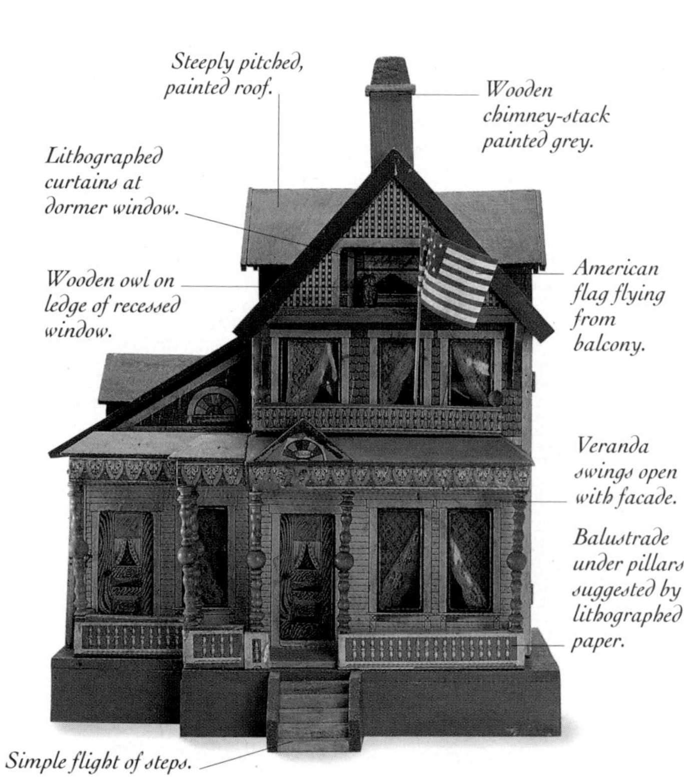

LOGO *(ABOVE)*

A Bliss logo appears twice on this house: on the lower panel of the front door and on the porch pediment.

GROUND FLOOR

The front door opens into the main room, furnished with only two items. An interior door leads to the kitchen, which also has a side entrance.

15cm (6in)

23cm (9in)

Lithograph-covered wood; hinged front and side wall.

THE FACADE

Bliss houses are renowned for the quality and detail of their lithographed exterior designs. This model, with its roofed veranda, recessed mock upper-storey window, and five-dormered roof, presents a complex facade that belies the simple interior.

PARLOUR FURNITURE *(ABOVE)* These two pieces are from a set of Bliss wooden furniture decorated with lithographed-paper; the set comprises four chairs, a piano, and a settee.

WASHINGTON DOLLS' HOUSE & TOY MUSEUM

The Interior

The four rooms are all papered with colourful modern patterns, with the additional attraction of *trompe l'oeil* fireplaces and doorways – a rather unexpected bonus in what seems, from the outside, to be a charming but fairly simple little bungalow. The wooden staircase leads to two low-ceilinged attics.

Wooden chimney-stack attached to rear roof section.

Fixed glazed window in attic.

Side of house hinged to open.

Compressed cardboard furniture by Moritz Gottschalk.

Trompe l'oeil *bathroom and doorway.*

Wooden staircase leads to attic.

Trompe l'oeil *fireplace in hall.*

SCHOENHUT BUNGALOW

American; made by A. Schoenhut of Philadelphia; 1917

ALBERT SCHOENHUT left Germany for the United States in 1867 at the age of 17. He was from a toy-making family in Wurttemberg, and continued the family tradition by founding a toy-making company in Philadelphia, Pennsylvania, in 1872. In 1917, when the firm was already well known for wooden dolls, circuses, and toy musical instruments, it introduced a new line, which was advertised as "High-class Dolls' Houses and Bungalows".

Schoenhut's miniature bungalows, which echoed a popular contemporary style of residence, became best-sellers. Unlike today's dolls' house manufacturers, the firm used architectural trends to advantage, emphasizing "the most modern style of paper hanging" in lithographed interiors, with many *trompe l'oeil* effects. This style changed in the mid-1920s when Schoenhut began to produce houses with shutters and window-boxes on the plain exterior walls, and no *trompe l'oeil* effects inside. Schoenhut toys have always been popular with children, and collectors today seem equally enthusiastic.

ILLUSIONS *(ABOVE)*
Schoenhut's catalogue promised "An illusion of a house full of fine rooms" – a promise fulfilled by this *trompe l'oeil* image of a room beyond the doorway.

Compressed cardboard roof embossed and painted to resemble shingles.

Hinged ridge of front roof section.

Lace curtains at fixed attic window.

Painted wooden window-frame around glazed window.

Real staircase made of wood.

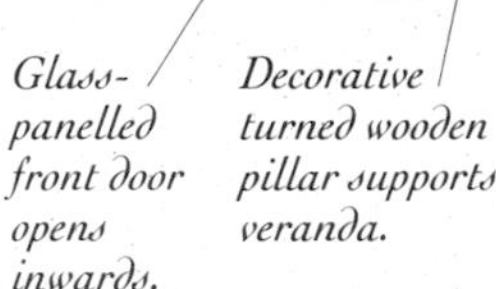

Glass-panelled front door opens inwards.

Decorative turned wooden pillar supports veranda.

THE FACADE
The bungalow has glazed windows in an embossed stone-effect front, and a balustraded porch. The red shingled roof has one central dormer window.

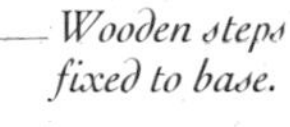

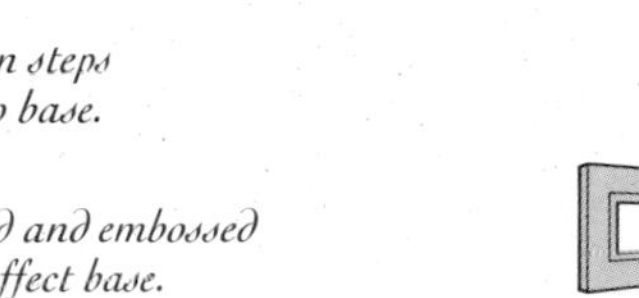

Wooden steps fixed to base.

Painted and embossed stone-effect base.

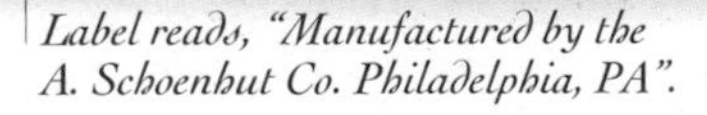

Label reads, "Manufactured by the A. Schoenhut Co. Philadelphia, PA".

58cm (23in)

50cm (20in)

Fixed front; both sides open; roof tilts back to reveal attic.

WASHINGTON DOLLS' HOUSE & TOY MUSEUM

HOBBIES HOUSE

English; made from Hobbies dolls' house plans; c.1926

SOME APPARENTLY IDENTICAL dolls' houses may not, in fact, have been commercially made. For many years monthly magazines produced by Hobbies of Dereham have included excellent plans for dolls' houses; once the plans were published many similar dolls' houses were successfully made at home by enthusiasts – often in secret, as a Christmas or birthday surprise for a child.

This particular design was originally meant for a 1:24 scale house, but it was enlarged to a size more suitable for a child. In 1926 Hobbies added furniture plans to their range; the pieces, designed for each room of the dolls' house, were cut from wood with a fretsaw. Later plans included instructions for a garage extension.

Chimney on side wall serves fire below.

Glazed windows, in fretworked frames.

Door and canopy made of varnished wood.

Hinged front door.

Metal press-stud represents doorbell.

Painted, curved wooden step.

THE FACADE
The exterior of the house is covered with papers supplied by Hobbies: a red-tiled roof, roughcast effect on the upper walls, and brickwork on the lower, reflecting the style of houses springing up in the English suburbs at the time.

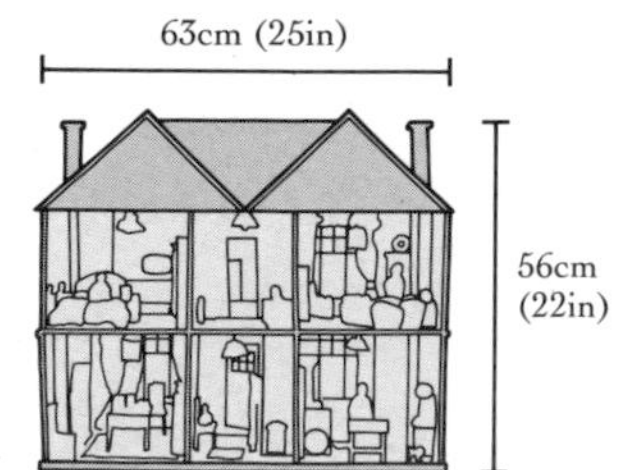

Paper-covered wood; open-back design; hinged door.

Hexagonal, wooden-framed mirror above fireplace.

Brass coal scuttle placed beside red brick-effect fireplace.

Wooden bookcase.

Printed roof-tile papers sold by Hobbies.

Block of wood, covered with brick-effect paper, forms chimney.

Gables suggest attic rooms, but roof is firmly fixed.

House equipped throughout with working electric lights.

First Floor

The first floor has a bedroom, bathroom, and living-room, all furnished with *c.*1920s and 1930s items and materials to represent the style of the period. The wooden bedroom furniture is by Elgin, who made dolls' house furniture from 1919 to 1926. A porcelain bath is just visible in the central bathroom.

German doll with wool-covered limbs and painted metal head, hands, and feet.

Ground Floor

A broom cupboard is built in underneath the stairs in the hall. Both the kitchen *(right)* and the dining-room *(left)* have fireplaces fitted to the chimney-breasts that extend down the end walls of the house.

Tile-effect wallpaper was often used in 1920s kitchens.

1930s metal gas cooker made by Taylor & Barrett of London.

Well-stocked broom cupboard fitted under stairs.

Thin but rigid wall.

Doll, with painted ceramic head, hands, and feet, wears original clothing.

Wooden "Pit-a-Pat" sink with metal taps, made by E. Lehman & Co.

HAMLEYS HOUSE

English; made by Lines Brothers; c.1929

LINES PRODUCED THIS INNOVATIVE DESIGN, with its imitation thatched roof (previous models had tiles) in 1929. It is an odd mixture of styles, with an "olde worlde" thatched roof and beams, and a modern garage incorporated into the structure. Although it became one of Lines' most popular models, to many young owners the lack of a designated kitchen in the house was infuriating, and most garages were probably converted, as in this example. The facade of the house is deceptive, hinting that there is an attic in addition to the garage and usual rooms. In fact there are only two main rooms, with a small one adjoining the bedroom. No bathroom or kitchen was provided, unless the landing and garage were adapted, as here. The house was strongly built, however, and the additional back opening made placing furniture in the deep main rooms easy. The front door and garage doors are both hinged to open. The house still bears the label indicating that it was made for sale by Hamleys Toyshop, London.

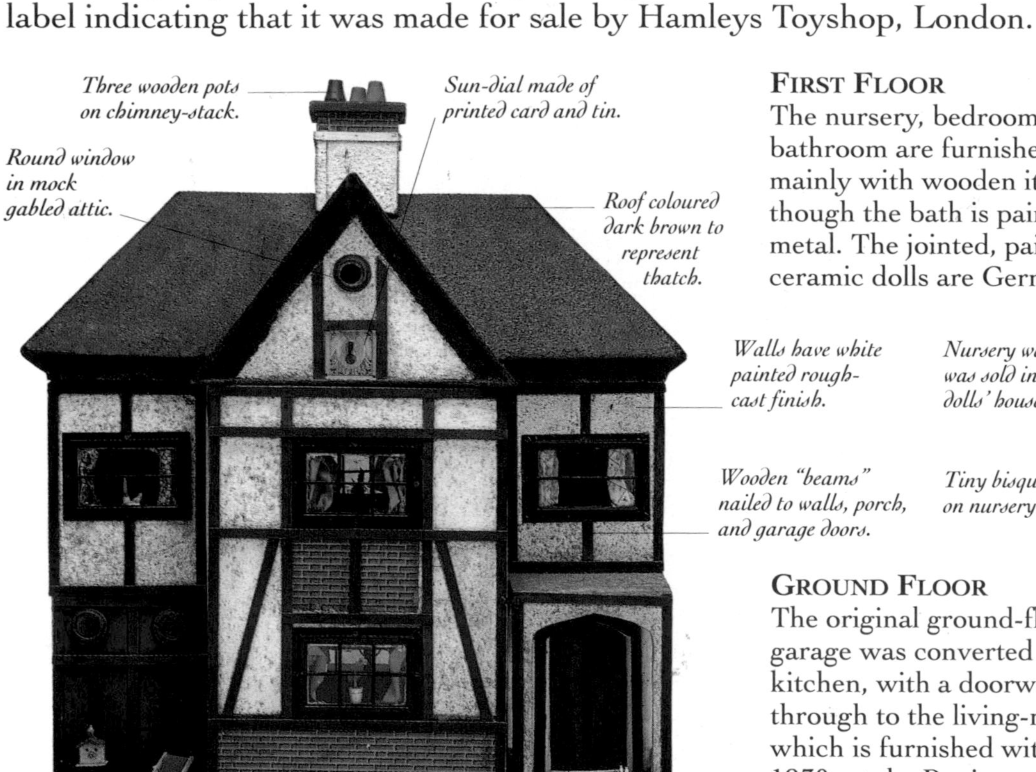

Three wooden pots on chimney-stack.

Sun-dial made of printed card and tin.

Round window in mock gabled attic.

Roof coloured dark brown to represent thatch.

Walls have white painted rough-cast finish.

Wooden "beams" nailed to walls, porch, and garage doors.

Label reads "Hamleys, 200–202 Regent Street, London W.1".

Wooden door with curved top and three vertical panels.

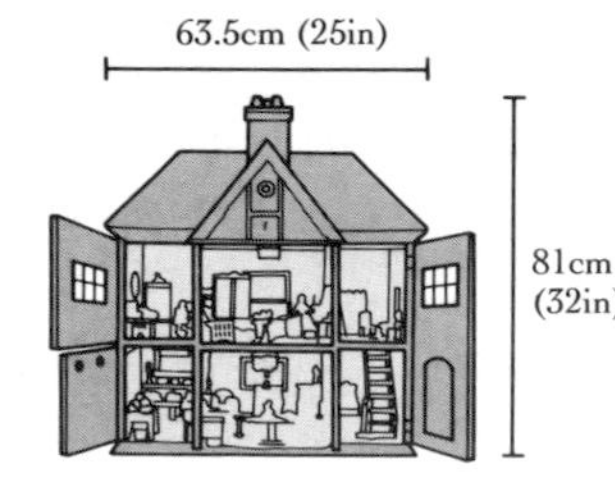

Facade hinged in four sections; back central section hinged.

FIRST FLOOR

The nursery, bedroom, and bathroom are furnished mainly with wooden items, though the bath is painted metal. The jointed, painted ceramic dolls are German.

Nursery wallpaper was sold in sheets for dolls' houses c.1930.

Tiny bisque doll on nursery table.

GROUND FLOOR

The original ground-floor garage was converted into a kitchen, with a doorway cut through to the living-room, which is furnished with a 1930s-style, Rexine-covered "Pit-a-Pat" three-piece suite made by E. Lehman & Co.

THE FACADE

Despite its unusual mixture of timbering, roughcast, brickwork, and thatch, plus built-in garage, this was one of Lines' most popular designs. Perhaps adult buyers saw it as reflecting the mock-Tudor style of houses being built in the developing English suburbs at the time.

Base of chimney-stack shaped to fit over roof and gable ridgepoles.

Gable with circular window and sun-dial unique to this model.

DESK *(RIGHT)*
On the varnished papier mâché desk, which was originally a wash-stand, are a glass blotter and ink-stand, red and black ink bottles, and a pen.

Hand-decorated book covers.

WIRELESS SETS *(BELOW)*
Wireless sets were a popular source of home entertainment in the 1930s. The simple wooden table-top model has printed details, while the radiogram (really a pencil sharpener) has paper decoration and dial.

1930s carpet-sweeper.

Painted wooden WC, pedestal basin, and chair.

Moulded plastic replica radiogram.

Printed dial and knobs.

Hinged top.

Replica of record made for Queen Mary's Dolls' House.

GRAMOPHONE *(ABOVE RIGHT)*
The metal gramophone has a movable turn-table, arm, and handle. The mid-1920s record (in its original "His Master's Voice" sleeve) plays the British national anthem.

CHURCH HILL HOUSE

English; made by Lines Brothers in 1939

TWENTIETH-CENTURY DOLLS' HOUSE designs generally appear to have been influenced more by the past than by contemporary styles of architecture. However, Lines Brothers did produce several "ultra-modern" designs with innovative features such as movable sun-traps and built-in garages that were popular at the time. Church Hill House was No. 52 in Lines' 1939 Tri-ang Toys Catalogue.

As the London home of the dolls' house owner was prepared for wartime living, so was the dolls' house, which was bought in a sale at Daniel Neale's London shoe-shop in January 1940 for 8s. 11d. With windows carefully taped over to prevent damage from flying glass, and other air-raid precautions, such as black-out curtains, the dolls' house and its family survived the war in London, where it still evokes 1940s life in the owner's childhood home.

Metal-framed window was added to balcony to provide a nursery.

THE FACADE

This house reflects the 1930s vogue for flat-roofed houses with simple facades. The typical 1930s colour scheme of cream and green, along with the metal window-frames, add to its authenticity, as does the air-raid shelter.

Movable chimney-stack serves fireplaces below.

Fashionable roof-top sun-parlour has open back.

Taped-over windows.

Anderson shelter home-made from silvered corrugated paper.

Wooden door with brass fittings opens inwards.

FIRST FLOOR

The bedroom was the only room upstairs until the balcony *(left)* was converted into a nursery. The buckets of sand on the landing and the heavy black-out curtains at the window were typical air-raid precautions.

Red and white gingham curtains at kitchen window.

GROUND FLOOR

Until the garage *(left)* was converted into a kitchen, the living-room was the only room on this floor. A bathroom was set up under the stairs, where the children's cots were also placed for protection.

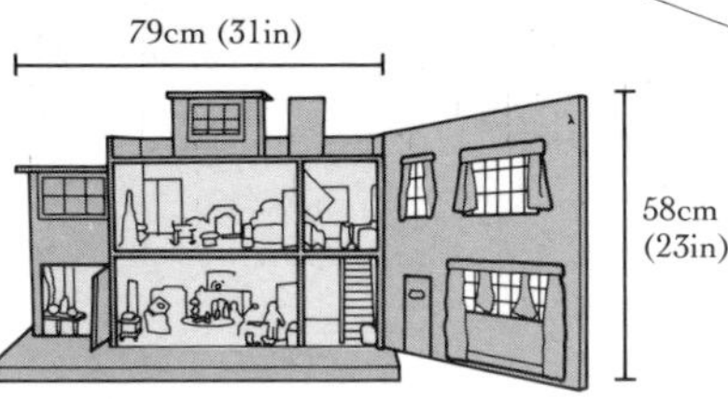

Wooden structure; hinged front and kitchen section.

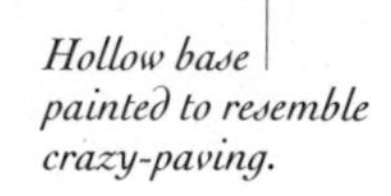
Hollow base painted to resemble crazy-paving.

Movable sun-parlour conceals electric battery.
Typical 1930s-style fireplace.
Air-raid warden on fire-watching duty, wears yellow "ARP" armband.
Wood and canvas garden chair.
Black-out curtains at side window.
Oil-lamp and assorted candles provide emergency lighting during power cuts.
Oval wooden dining-table and chairs by Pit-a-Pat.
Post-war telephone temporarily replaces missing original.
Childrens' cots, placed under stairs for protection during air-raids, hide bath and WC in makeshift bathroom.

1940s Furnishings

The pit-a-pat furniture in the living-room and kitchen of Church Hill House still has the original price labels attached; the dining-room table, for example, cost 1s 3d, while the chairs cost 8d each. Other commercially made items include a metal wireless-set and tea-trolley, and a Dol-Toi refrigerator. All the wooden bedroom furniture was made by David Davis, the fiancé of the family's cook. The young dolls' house owner made the lace-trimmed cot under the stairs as well as the other nursery furniture.

Handle of painted metal oil-stove is movable.

Metal plate-rack is adjustable and removable.

Painted metal egg in metal frying-pan.

Hinged oven door is removable.

Oil Heater *(above)*
The metal replica stove heats the bedroom, where the fire-screen hides an empty hearth.

Gas Stove *(above/right)*
The gas stove, by Taylor & Barrett, is of white painted metal, with unpainted door and gas-rings, and a black plate-rack – typical 1930s colouring. Because of food rationing, the oven is empty, and only one precious egg is "frying" in the pan.

Printed cotton tray-cloth is one of set.

Trolley *(right)*
The metal trolley, with movable wheels and a "brass" handle, is spray-painted in two shades of green. Underneath it is marked "Foreign", indicating that it was imported.

Dressing Table *(above)*
Made from scraps of wood, this varnished dressing-table has one drawer that can be pulled out with the aid of two carved wooden handles.

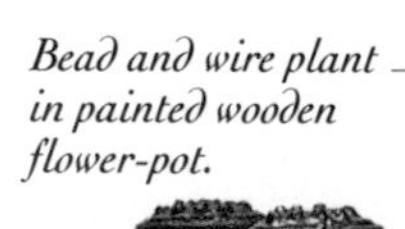

Kitchen Units *(below)*
All three pieces are made of painted wood; both the sink and basin have metal taps. The mid-1940s refrigerator still bears its "Dol-Toi Refrigerator" label.

WAR-TIME DOLLS

ALL FOUR DOLLS in this house are German-made, ceramic, and jointed at the shoulders and hips (except for the child in the blue wooden cot who has no hip joints). They are typical of dolls from the 1930s that bridged the gap between the earlier delicate bisque models and the post-war plastic variety. Unlike their bisque forerunners, which were finely moulded with painting restricted to the facial features and the hair, these dolls' faces and hands are less well defined, and they are painted all over. Many similar dolls came in sets, dressed as family members or as uniformed staff, but others, like these examples, were bought singly.

FEMALE DOLL *(LEFT)*
This doll originally wore a dress, but she was reclothed in a "siren-suit", a practical one-piece garment that was popular during the war (this is a copy of one worn by the owner's mother). She also carries a miniature home-made gas-mask.

GAS-MASK, RATION BOOKS, AND IDENTITY CARD *(RIGHT)* The gas-mask, of paper, talc, and tape, is a genuine war-time model. The two ration books and the blue identity card are later replicas of originals, now missing from the house.

MALE DOLL *(BELOW)*
It was beyond the owner's skill to copy her father's army uniform, so the male doll became an air-raid warden instead. The suit, collar, and tie were his original outfit, but the "ARP" (Air Raid Protection) arm-band and helmet were home-made.

MODERN HOUSE

English; designed and made by Christopher Cole in the 1970s

ALTHOUGH BOTH CRAFTSMEN and commercial firms have produced a great deal of excellent new miniature furniture, often replicas of contemporary pieces, very few dolls' houses have been made in designs reflecting modern architecture. This extremely unusual 1970s example was an early design by Dr Christopher Cole, a general practitioner who began making dolls' houses, partly out of his keen interest in architecture, and partly because he wished to have a hobby that he could develop into a full-time occupation when he retired.

The house, which was sold as a kit, is constructed of lightly varnished birch plywood, with a long side window panel and front door made of clear plastic. It has removable floors, and pegged interior walls and stairs, designed to allow children to create differently shaped rooms within a firm basic structure, thus stimulating imaginative play. Children proved to be more conventional than anticipated, however, preferring traditional-looking dolls' houses, so Christopher Cole altered his plans, and relatively few houses like this were ever produced.

Window panels incorporated into basic structural design.

Floors planned to be seen through window panels.

Entrance hall has plastic, plate-glass-effect door and panel.

Red dye-cast metal 1949-style "Coccinelle Berline" Volkswagen, made by French firm Solido.

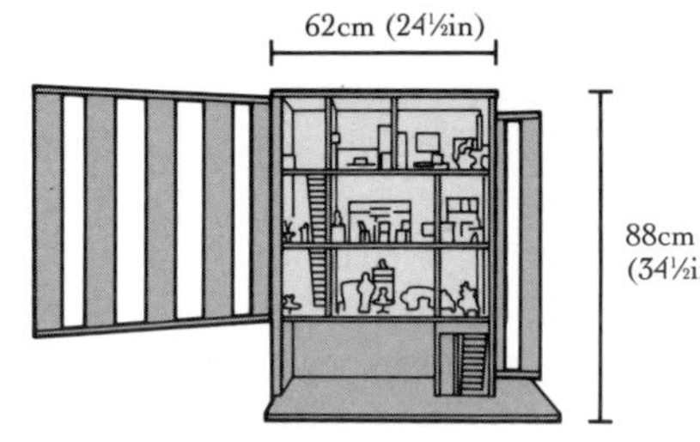

Wood and plastic; hinged facade and side panel.

THE FACADE

Clear plastic strips between wooden panels, crossed by the horizontal lines of the floors, form a striking facade on this representation of a modern four-storeyed building. The area below the house is left open, for use as a shop or carport, as the owner wishes.

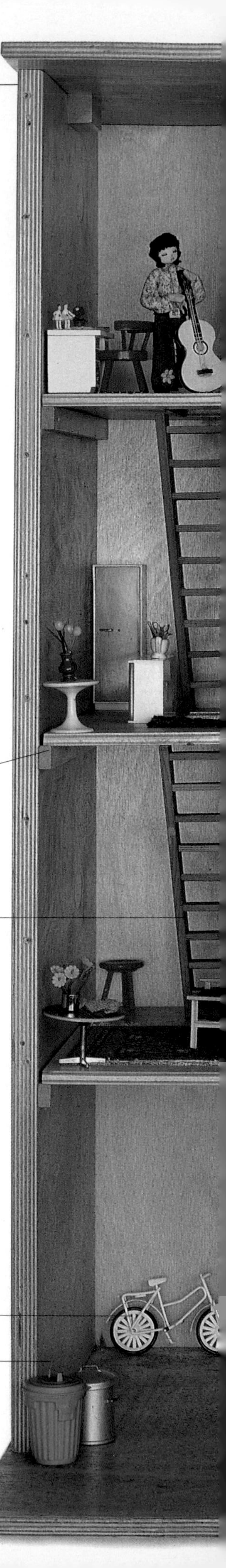

Floor supported by strips of wood on interior side walls.

On first and second floors, stairs peg into holes on left side interior walls.

Painted metal bicycle with rubber wheels, made in China c.1950.

Open front area, used here as carport.

Opening side window extends from roof to ground level.
External and internal walls are of plain varnished plywood.
Inner walls peg into holes in floors.
Plastic and metal chair by Brio.
Floor designed to slide out of framework.
Television, bookcase, and record-player by Lundby.
Stairs from ground floor emerge on landing.
Pegs on right side wall hold first flight of stairs.
Black plastic strip on door provides handle.
Base wider on right side to accommodate opening side panel.
Firm base provides essential support for this type of house.

THIRD FLOOR
The bathroom *(centre)*, with hinged doors to the rooms on either side, is fitted with Lundby units, while the main bedroom *(right)* contains a selection of wood and plastic pieces. The landing on the left is furnished as a teenager's "pad" with furniture made by Hansi.

SECOND FLOOR
The interior walls have been moved to provide a large dining-room between the landing *(left)* and the small kitchen *(right)*. The Scandinavian furniture is mainly plastic, with some wooden items in the kitchen, including a kitchen unit by the Danish firm Hansi; the wood-effect shelving unit in the dining-room is by Brio.

FIRST FLOOR
There is only one room on this floor as the stairs, oddly, switch from the right side to the left, creating a landing on either side of the living-room. The internal walls have archways connecting the landings and living-room, which is fitted with furniture made by Brio.

GROUND FLOOR
The entrance hall *(right)* has a clear plastic plate-glass-effect front panel and a hinged door. A Volkswagen "Beetle" is parked in the open space, along with a bicycle and two dustbins.

SCANDINAVIAN STYLE

THE FURNITURE in Christopher Cole's 1970s-style house was chosen to represent the type of contemporary designs that a busy professional family might have chosen during that period. Most of the pieces are Scandinavian, made by the Swedish firms Lundby and Brio, and by the Danish firm Hansi. Hansi products were mostly made of wood, with some fabric. Lundby, too, produced wooden furniture but, like Brio, they also made some excellent miniature replicas of modern items, using moulded plastics.

Daisies in plastic jug.

Moulded plastic and metal chair.

Wooden tea-set is German.

Miniature replica plastic coffee-maker.

English-made wooden table.

TABLE AND CHAIR *(ABOVE)* On the plain wooden table are a realistic miniature replica coffee-maker and plastic jug of flowers by Lundby; the plastic and metal chair was made by Brio.

Miniature replica of contemporary furniture, made by Brio.

Goblet, vase, and plastic table with flocked top all by Lundby.

Red-flocked armchair swivels on metal base.

Contemporary use of metal in furniture reflected by Brio miniatures.

SOFA AND CHAIR *(LEFT)* In the 1970s and 80s, influenced by the designer Arne Jacobsen, Brio made some replicas of modern furniture. The red sofa and armchair are two famous examples.

BATHROOM UNITS *(BELOW/RIGHT)* Lundby have produced dolls' house furniture and miniatures since the 1950s. These units illustrate their attention to detail, with well-designed, realistic accessories.

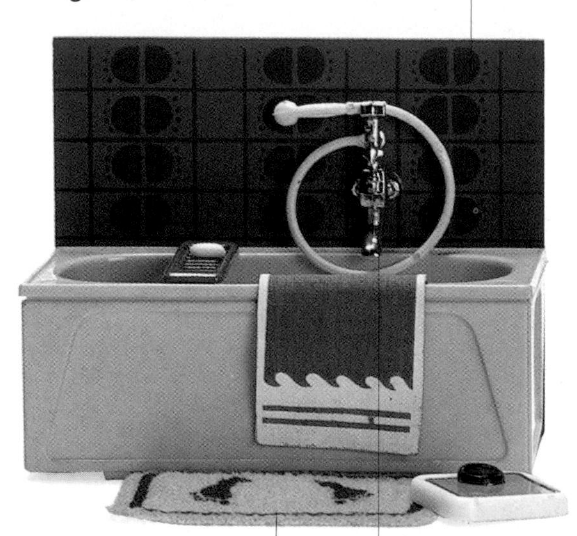

Bath unit has integral tiled wall section.

Bathroom set includes bath-mats, scales, and soap-rack.

Bath has shower attachment and other accessories.

Realistic shower cabinet is part of bathroom set.

Shower unit matches bath in co-ordinated bathroom set.

Detailed realistic tooth-brushes, tooth-mugs, and soap.

"His 'n' her" basins in bathroom unit.

Plastic "electric" razor plugged into socket.

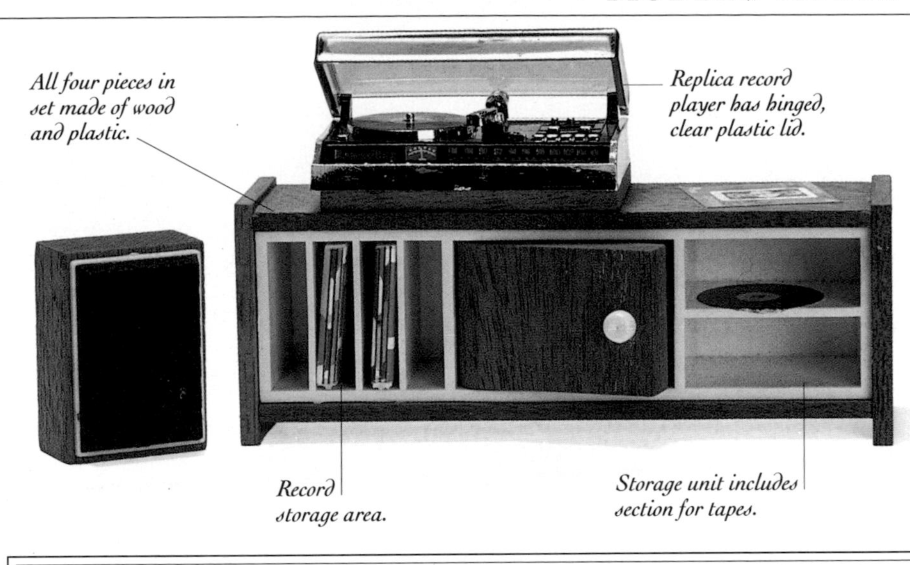
All four pieces in set made of wood and plastic.
Replica record player has hinged, clear plastic lid.
Miniature "stereophonic" loudspeaker.
Record storage area.
Storage unit includes section for tapes.
Moulded plastic gives mesh effect at front of loudspeaker.

RECORD PLAYER AND STORAGE UNIT *(LEFT)*
The meticulous attention to detail makes these items highly realistic. Many of the parts are movable: for example the arm of the authentic-looking record player can be moved from rest to play position.

A TYPICAL 1970s FAMILY

THE DOLLS' HOUSE OWNER, who intended to record contemporary fashions as well as furnishing trends, commissioned these dolls from Barbara Cox, who designed and made them with flexible bodies and limbs, embroidered stockinette-covered features, and wool hair. After consultations about the dolls' characters, they were then dressed appropriately. The family consists of a father, visualized as a television producer, the mother (an author), her retired father, a teenage son, two young children (boy and girl twins), and a baby; an au pair is also included in the household. Only four members of the family are shown here – father, mother, teenage son, and the au pair.

Father wears fashionable polo-necked sweater and suede jacket and trousers.
Only jacket is removable.
Au pair knits with yellow wool on steel pins.
Teenage son wears "flower-power" shirt and flared jeans.
Wool hair and embroidered features.
Mother wears suede jacket and velvet trouser-suit.
Flexible dolls can hold any chosen position.
Au pair wears high boots and mini-skirt.
Blue version of Brio chairs.

PLAYMOBIL HOUSE

German; first produced by Geobra Brandstätter in 1989

THE BRANDSTATTER COMPANY started making toys in the 1930s, its best known lines being the Hula Hoop (1958) and Playmobil toys (1974). The dolls' house, launched in 1989 as part of The Good Old Days series, was aimed specifically at girls, as the firm's other lines were played with mostly by boys. The company chose a turn-of-the-century-style house that it believed would appeal to children. Maintaining the German tradition that toys are educational, Geobra Brandstätter designed decor and accessories that convey the period atmosphere, and figures from different walks of life, allowing children to role play and to gain an insight into life during a different period.

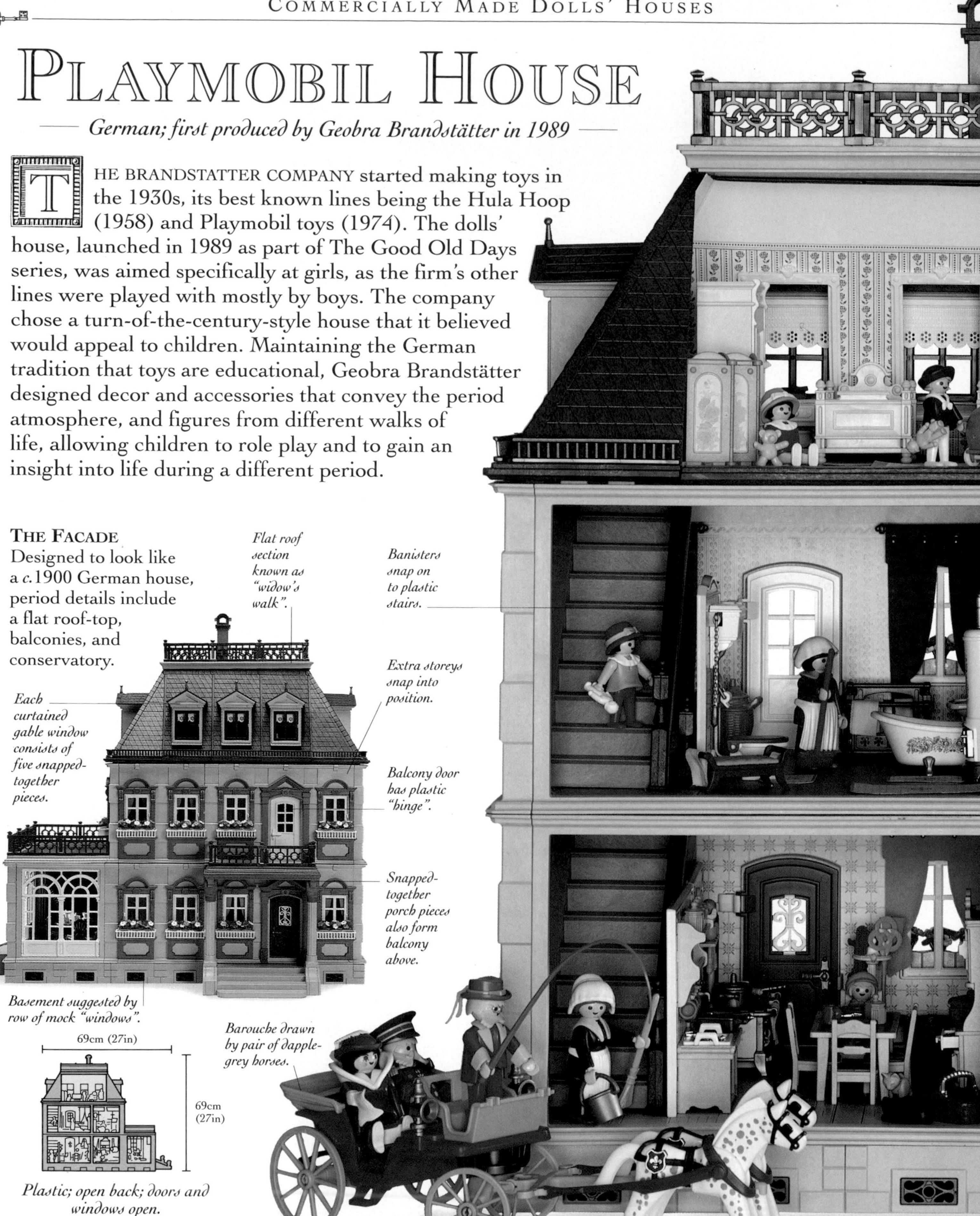

THE FACADE Designed to look like a *c.*1900 German house, period details include a flat roof-top, balconies, and conservatory.

Plastic; open back; doors and windows open.

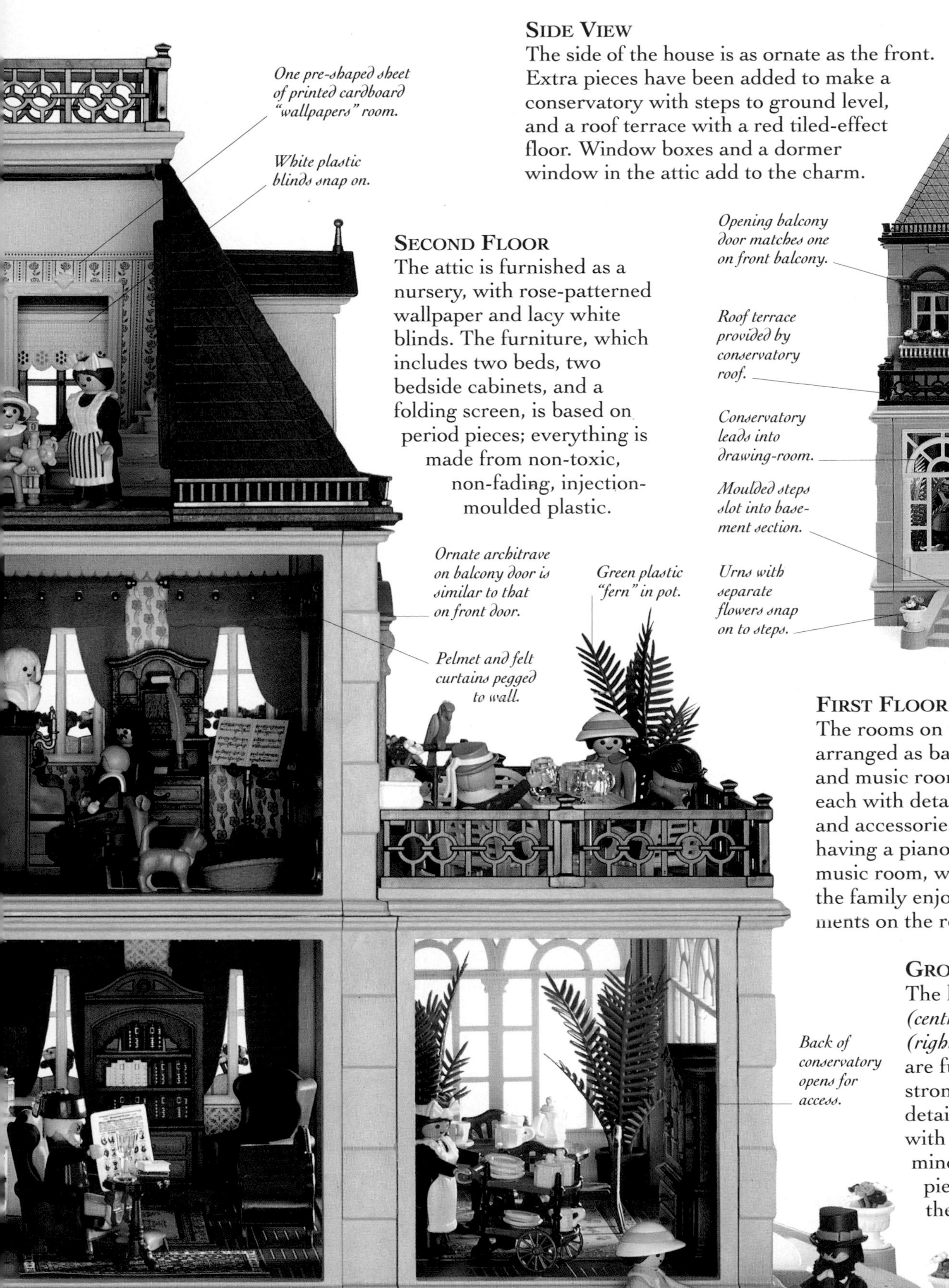

One pre-shaped sheet of printed cardboard "wallpapers" room.

White plastic blinds snap on.

SIDE VIEW
The side of the house is as ornate as the front. Extra pieces have been added to make a conservatory with steps to ground level, and a roof terrace with a red tiled-effect floor. Window boxes and a dormer window in the attic add to the charm.

Sloping roof sections slot together.

Opening balcony door matches one on front balcony.

Roof terrace provided by conservatory roof.

Conservatory leads into drawing-room.

Moulded steps slot into basement section.

Urns with separate flowers snap on to steps.

SECOND FLOOR
The attic is furnished as a nursery, with rose-patterned wallpaper and lacy white blinds. The furniture, which includes two beds, two bedside cabinets, and a folding screen, is based on period pieces; everything is made from non-toxic, non-fading, injection-moulded plastic.

Ornate architrave on balcony door is similar to that on front door.

Green plastic "fern" in pot.

Pelmet and felt curtains pegged to wall.

FIRST FLOOR
The rooms on this floor are arranged as bathroom *(left)* and music room *(right)*, each with detailed units and accessories. A child is having a piano lesson in the music room, while some of the family enjoy refreshments on the roof terrace.

GROUND FLOOR
The kitchen *(left)*, study *(centre)*, and conservatory *(right)* on the ground floor are furnished with bright, strongly made, realistically detailed pieces, all designed with young children in mind. Many of the smaller pieces can be gripped in the dolls' vice-like hands where appropriate.

Back of conservatory opens for access.

Perambulator has movable wheels – and occupant.

playmobil 1900

PLASTIC FURNISHINGS

MOST PLAYMOBIL FURNITURE is sold in room-set packs with accessories included. Items from the bathroom, kitchen, and music-room sets are featured here. Some pieces, like the piano, are free-standing, while others are fixed to wall-units. Almost all the items are made of injection-moulded plastic, but there are also some fabric accessories such as felt curtains with pelmets, bathroom towels, and printed composition rugs.

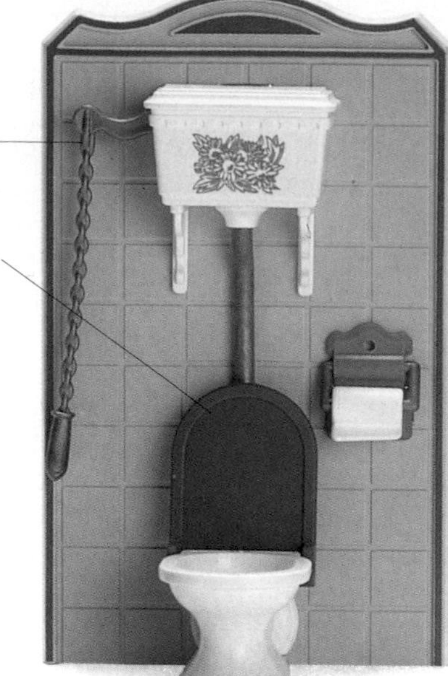

Movable chain on cistern.

WC has hinged lid.

Printed paper mat around base of WC.

Gilt lamp and mirror above basin.

BATHROOM UNITS *(ABOVE)*
Both bathroom units shown here are designed to provide extra walls if required. The lavatory seat and chain are both movable, and the set includes printed paper mats, a bath, stove, and towel-rail.

MUSIC SET *(BELOW)*
The piano plays *Für Elise* when the keys are pressed. The set includes a music-stand and music teacher.

Playmobil head incorporated into luminous bust.

"Gilt" candle in sconce.

Miniature Beethoven score.

"Schimmel" piano with hinged lid.

Revolving red seat on piano stool.

KITCHEN UNITS *(BELOW)*
Both units are fixed to wall plates, and include movable accessories such as the mugs and plates in the shelves by the sink. Two "copper" pans sit on the stove, above which is a rack of kitchen utensils.

Utensils include rolling-pin and fish-slice.

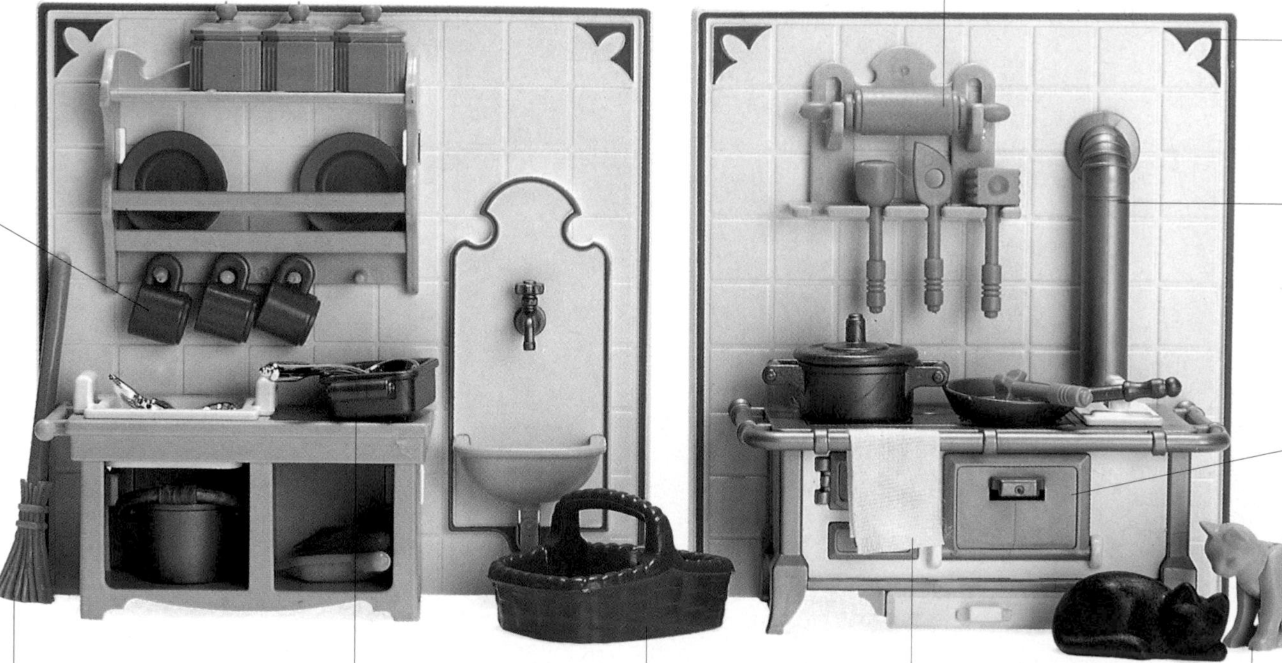

Orange mug hangs from shelf unit.

Back plate provides extra wall if necessary.

Fixed pipe runs from stove to back wall-plate.

Door of kitchen stove opens.

Yellow plastic broom is part of kitchen set.

Tray of "silver" cutlery on draining-board.

Kitchen basket made of moulded plastic.

White fabric towel hanging on rail.

Grey cat has movable head.

PLAYMOBIL FAMILY AND STAFF

PLAYMOBIL DOLLS are designed to be safe and easy for young children to hold, attractively colourful, and without any sharp edges. They have no mechanical parts, but the heads are movable and the dolls can stand, sit, and hold objects in their vice-like hands, allowing children to develop and use their imagination to the full as they play. The dolls were designed by Hans Beck, who was influenced by children's drawings of people. As it is company policy that all the dolls' faces must look alike, Herr Beck developed a pattern suitable for all the characters portrayed, using simple round heads with dots for eyes and a curve for the mouth. These features are moulded, not painted on, so they will not rub off.

Bearded coachman wears spectacles and blue hat.

Housemaid's cap is removable.

Parlour maid in afternoon uniform.

THE STAFF *(RIGHT)* The costumes worn by the coachman and the three maids are more colourful than strictly accurate for 1900, but their design does successfully suggest the period.

Tea-trolley, laden with "china", has moving wheels.

Coachman wears breeches and red knee-high boots.

EXTENDED FAMILY *(BELOW)* All three generations have the same Playmobil body design; the children are simply smaller versions, first introduced in 1981 by Geobra Brandstätter.

Second housemaid wears morning uniform.

Hands swivel at wrists to grasp trolley.

Arms jointed at shoulders.

Grandfather wears removable smoking-cap.

Musician holds removable quill pen.

Small boy wears green cravat.

Family parrot can be removed from perch.

Logo can be seen on base of little girl's foot.

Design allows doll to bend at waist.

DOLLS' HOUSE CAROUSEL *(LEFT)* *A modern example of an old favourite – a pop-up book that provides a two-storey, eight-roomed dolls' house, complete with a fold-up staircase and opening doors and cupboards.*

MINIATURE "BLISS" DOLLS' HOUSE *(RIGHT)* *Made in the United States, this modern paper version of a Bliss-type dolls' house has external features printed on. The open back reveals two rooms.*

faithfully reproduced in miniature as a child's plaything. A completely different use of natural unpainted wood is demonstrated by architectural student Jane Blyth with her imaginative creation, the Weavers' House *(see pp.116–17)*. Jane described the necessary materials for her most unusual structures as being "space, light, and shade"; wood seems almost to be an afterthought.

— HISTORICAL DIMENSIONS —

Wood was all important, though, to Henry Hall, the Master Mariner who built and furnished Contented Cot *(see pp.114–115)* for his baby daughter in 1886. To have such a special dolls' house must have delighted the little girl later on, as her father pasted the newspaper announcement of her birth over the attic window, and also carved his initials on some of the furniture.

Unfortunately, we do not know if Contented Cot is a miniature version of the Halls' own cottage, but there is another dolls' house, still under construction, that is an exact replica of a real London home. It has features such as stained-glass windows, metal "cast-iron" balusters, plaster mouldings, cornices, and friezes, as well as the external iron-work and balustrades, all created as exact 1:12 replicas of the originals *(see p.134)*. The miniature house is intended to be a record of a family home during three generations' occupancy, providing a very unusual three-dimensional "document".

Unusual dolls' houses on a grand scale include magnificent buildings such as the Queen Mary's Dolls' House, in Windsor Castle, England, and Titania's Palace, in Legoland, Denmark. The Fairy Castle of Colleen Moore, which is displayed in Chicago's Museum of Science and Industry, is a wonderful fantasy, realized by the best of Hollywood's artists and imaginative craftsmen.

The revival of interest in miniature houses, which have been designed and built for adults to decorate and furnish with beautiful artefacts, has resulted in a number of unique houses being created for today's collectors – particularly those in the United Kingdom and the United States.

Some English stately homes, which do not have an heirloom miniature house to display, are showing wonderful modern examples that have

JAPANESE NESTING HOUSES *(LEFT) These five, small box-like houses, of stained and printed wood, fit into each other like the better-known Russian Matryoshka dolls.*

been created and furnished by highly skilled artist-craftsmen. Two such makers of miniature buildings with especially fine interior decoration and furniture are John Hodgson and Kevin Mulvaney. John Hodgson has produced a series of period residences for display at Hever Castle, Edenbridge, Kent, England, while two of Kevin Mulvaney's creations have travelled far and wide: Britannia House tours to raise funds for the African Medical Research Foundation, and another model, based on a wing of Versailles, was bought by the Californian Angels' Attic Museum. It is also used to raise funds for charity.

— DOLLS' HOUSE OCCUPANTS —

Sometimes beautiful buildings have very unusual occupants. Colleen Moore's Castle and Titania's Palace were designed for invisible elves and fairies, while Mirror Grange was a home built for Pip, Squeak, and Wilfred – a dog, penguin, and rabbit who appeared daily in a cartoon in a British newspaper during the 1920s and 30s. This fascinating "house on a rock", which was designed by Maxwell Ayrton, also raised funds for charity.

Coming down to earth, or rather to the level of the nursery floor, unusual dwellings for dolls have often been popular toys. During the 1920s and 1930s, some interesting wooden "mobile-homes" were produced, including caravans and even a houseboat on invisible wheels *(see pp.118–19)*. Two modern equivalents of these are now available: Mattel's Barbie doll has an ingeniously designed mobile home, while the Sylvanian animals inhabit a canal narrow-boat. Both of these toys are plastic.

Children and adults have always been fascinated by tiny things. At the turn of the century "The Smallest" series of rooms in a matchbox was produced *(see p.111)*; today, plastic versions are advertised as "pocket-sized playmates". Of course, dolls' house nurseries must have their own dolls' houses and a number of these are available, ranging from plastic models and reproduction Bliss-type printed cardboard designs to limited editions, made from thin painted wood or card.

It really goes without saying that, for the makers of dolls' houses that can be grouped into a category named "unusual", the range and scope is almost unlimited. They certainly seem to have used every possible – and sometimes seemingly impossible – material when constructing them.

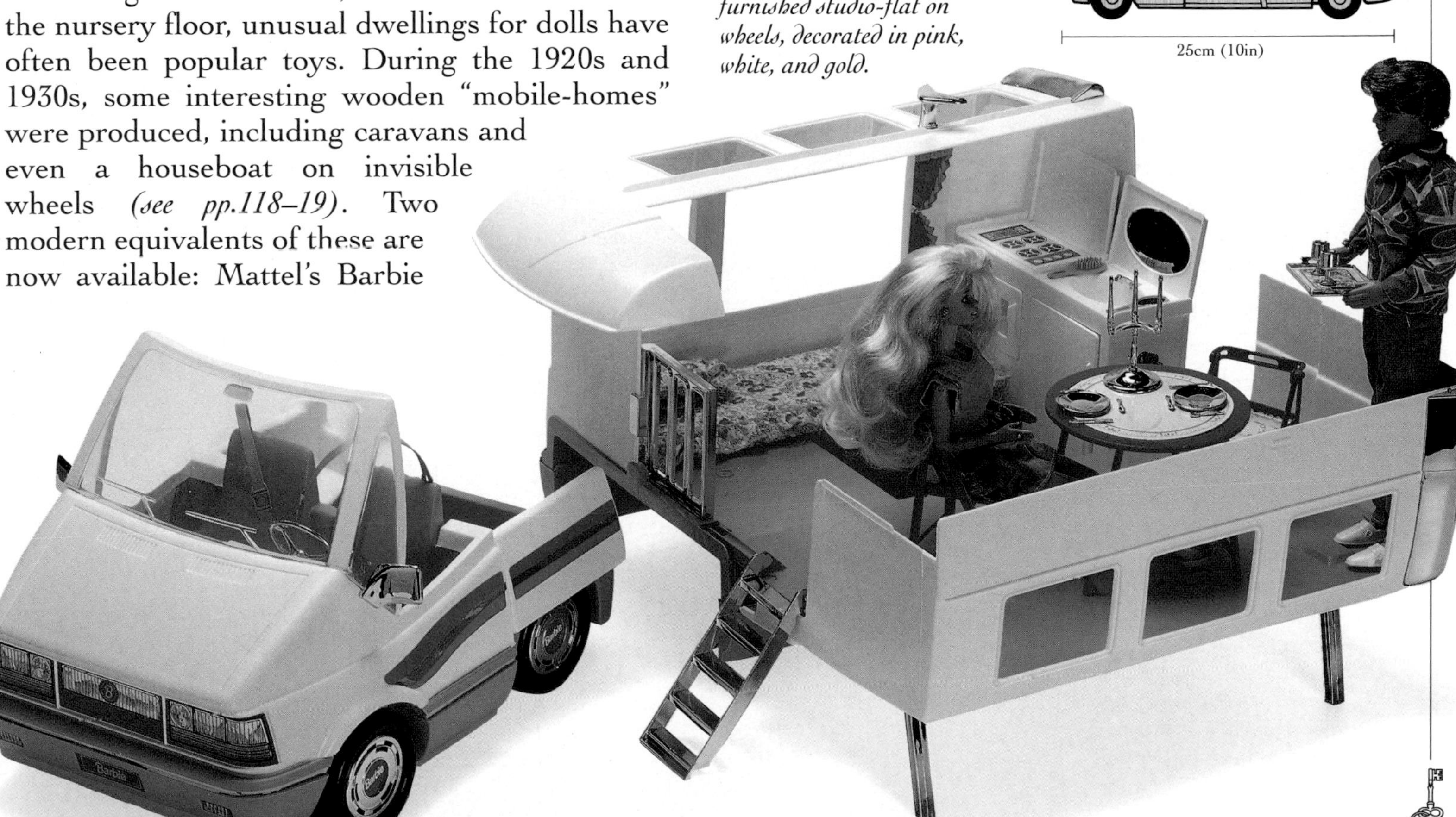

BARBIE'S MOBILE HOME *(BELOW) The ingenious design of Barbie's mobile home allows the vehicle to open into two sections; it provides Barbie with a fully furnished studio-flat on wheels, decorated in pink, white, and gold.*

Attic Studio

Part of the back roof, with a skylight, is hinged, revealing the artist at work in his studio. A newspaper cutting pasted above the dormer window announces the birth of Henry Hall's daughter in 1886.

Metal bar across front of high-chair is removable.

Dining chair, made by Henry Hall as part of dining-room set.

Henry Hall's initials carved on piano.

Piano and Chairs

(ABOVE) The furniture is simply and sturdily made, but Henry Hall's artistic skill is revealed by his use of gilt decoration and the piano's fretwork motif. The balloon-backed high-chair matches the dining chairs.

Artist doll dressed in smock and floppy hat, works at painting on easel.

Slate-tiled-effect horizontal roof sections fit together when closed.

Sand shaken over newly painted walls gives roughcast effect.

Wallpapers, carpet, and curtain materials all date from c.1880s.

Carved wooden mantelpiece with small metal fender.

China-headed doll with bisque limbs and soft body.

Grooves in floor and ceiling allow back wall section to slide out.

Painted, carved wood and wire light fixture.

Mirror in gilded frame hangs above mantelpiece.

Dining-room carpet made from Victorian petit-point bag.

CONTENTED COT

English; made by Devonshire sea-captain in 1886

WITH ITS NAME, DATE, MAKER, and first owner all recorded in or on its structure, this is one of the few dolls' houses with a known provenance. As well as the name above the door and the date over the attic window, a newspaper cutting announcing the "Birth ... October 11th at Mount Pleasant Road, Brixham (Devon), wife of Henry Hall, Master Mariner, of a daughter" is pasted inside the attic. Unfortunately the first name of the daughter, for whom the house was made, is unknown. Much of the original furniture remains, some marked "H.H."; other pieces of furniture and dolls have been added, all of the same period and scale. The present owner hopes that research will reveal if the dolls' house resembles the Brixham home of Henry Hall, the house's talented creator.

Small wooden sash window glides smoothly up and down in frame.

China-headed maid, with bisque limbs and soft body, wears original morning uniform.

FIRST FLOOR
The upper room is furnished as a bed-sitting-room, with a simple wooden bed, a carved chaise longue, and an upholstered settee. A door behind the fixed wall leads to the stairs.

House name carved above door.

Lever outside front door activates bell in attic.

Back door fixed; all other doors and windows (except attic skylight) open.

Chimney-stack serves two fireplaces below.

Front roof is fixed.

Hinged, double casement windows open inwards.

Panels of perforated tin attached to wooden rail form balcony.

Extended base forms walkway around house.

Sea shells decorate base.

GROUND FLOOR
The ground floor comprises a dining-room, hall, and stairs that are visible only through the opened front door. One section of the back wall, with painted back door, is fixed; the other section slides out to give access.

THE FACADE
"Contented Cot" is carved in a curve over the front door, complementing the window arches. The wood and metal balcony, carved finials, ridgepole, and gabled attic window, illustrate the maker's skill and artistry; the sand-covered walls and sea-shell ornamentation are clues to his maritime past.

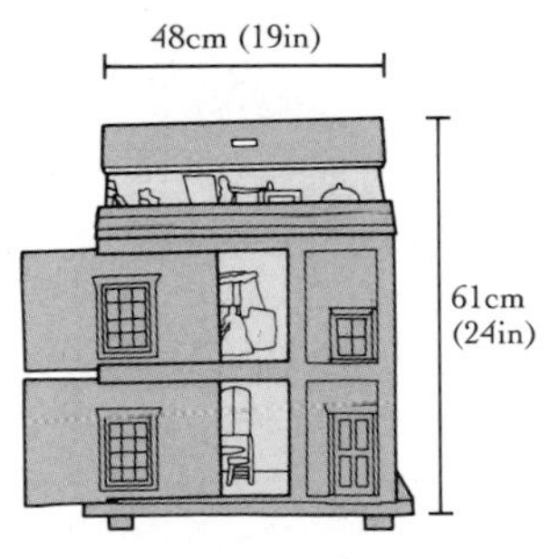

Two sliding panels in back; rear roof section hinged.

WEAVERS' HOUSE

English; designed and made by Jane Blyth; c.1970

THIS HOUSE IS A PARADOX: designed as a child's toy, yet it intrigues adults. It is a modern structure, solid enough for active play, but capable of changing shape. Perhaps a clue lies in the words of its creator who expects it to be "taken to pieces without falling apart". Jane Blyth wanted the house to be a toy that would stimulate creative play and that children would enjoy.

The house has a conventionally shaped roof, but otherwise its construction depends on the imagination of the owner. Although the house can be formed into complex patterns, it is made from simple and easily found materials – lolly sticks, dowelling, string, pieces of linen, clothes pegs, etc. Since making her first houses, Jane Blyth has created several other "theme" houses and entered a multi-cultural crib/house for the competition run by *Architectural Design* magazine in 1983.

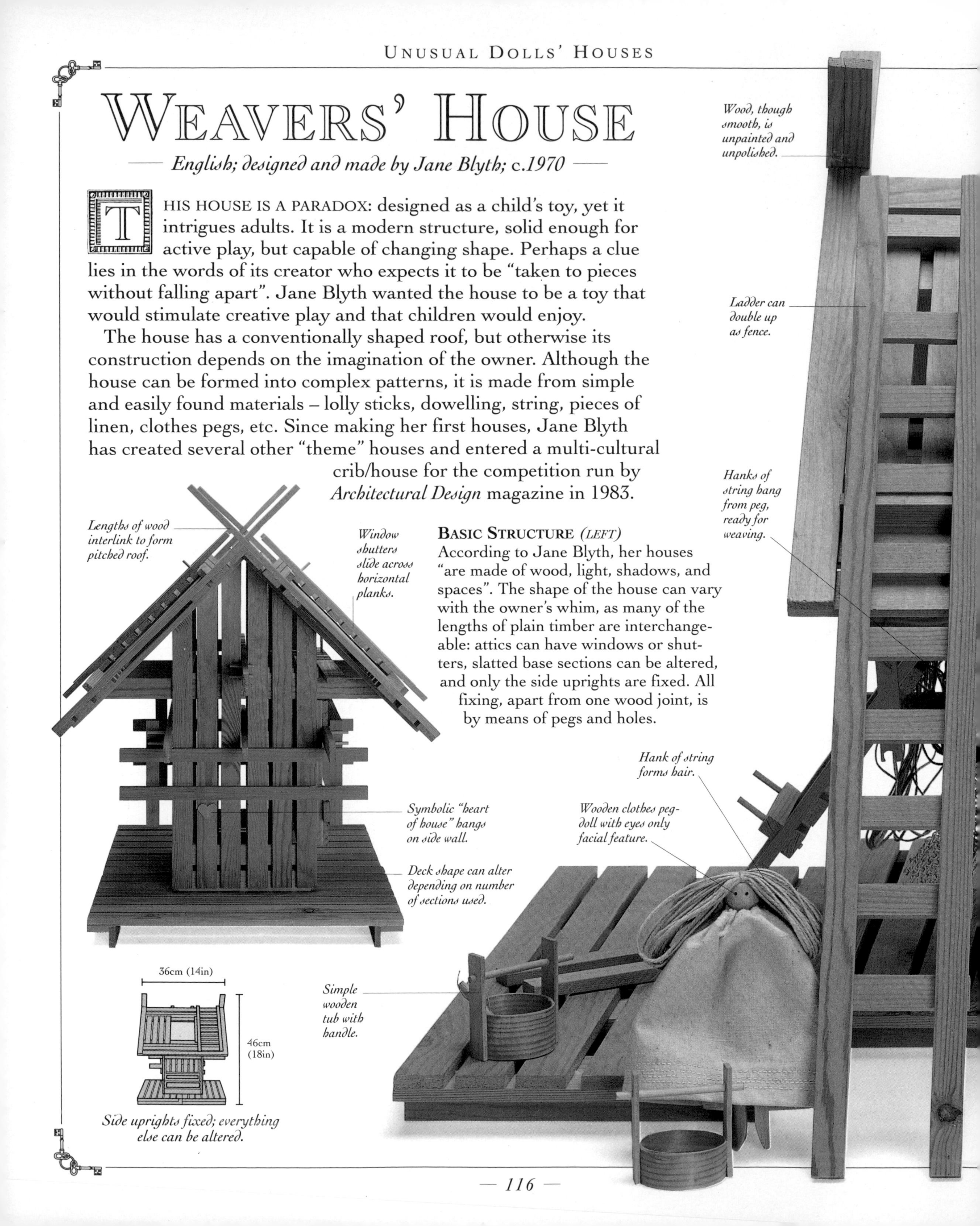

Wood, though smooth, is unpainted and unpolished.
Ladder can double up as fence.
Hanks of string hang from peg, ready for weaving.
Lengths of wood interlink to form pitched roof.
Window shutters slide across horizontal planks.
Symbolic "heart of house" hangs on side wall.
Deck shape can alter depending on number of sections used.
Hank of string forms hair.
Wooden clothes peg-doll with eyes only facial feature.
Simple wooden tub with handle.
36cm (14in)
46cm (18in)

BASIC STRUCTURE *(LEFT)*
According to Jane Blyth, her houses "are made of wood, light, shadows, and spaces". The shape of the house can vary with the owner's whim, as many of the lengths of plain timber are interchangeable: attics can have windows or shutters, slatted base sections can be altered, and only the side uprights are fixed. All fixing, apart from one wood joint, is by means of pegs and holes.

Side uprights fixed; everything else can be altered.

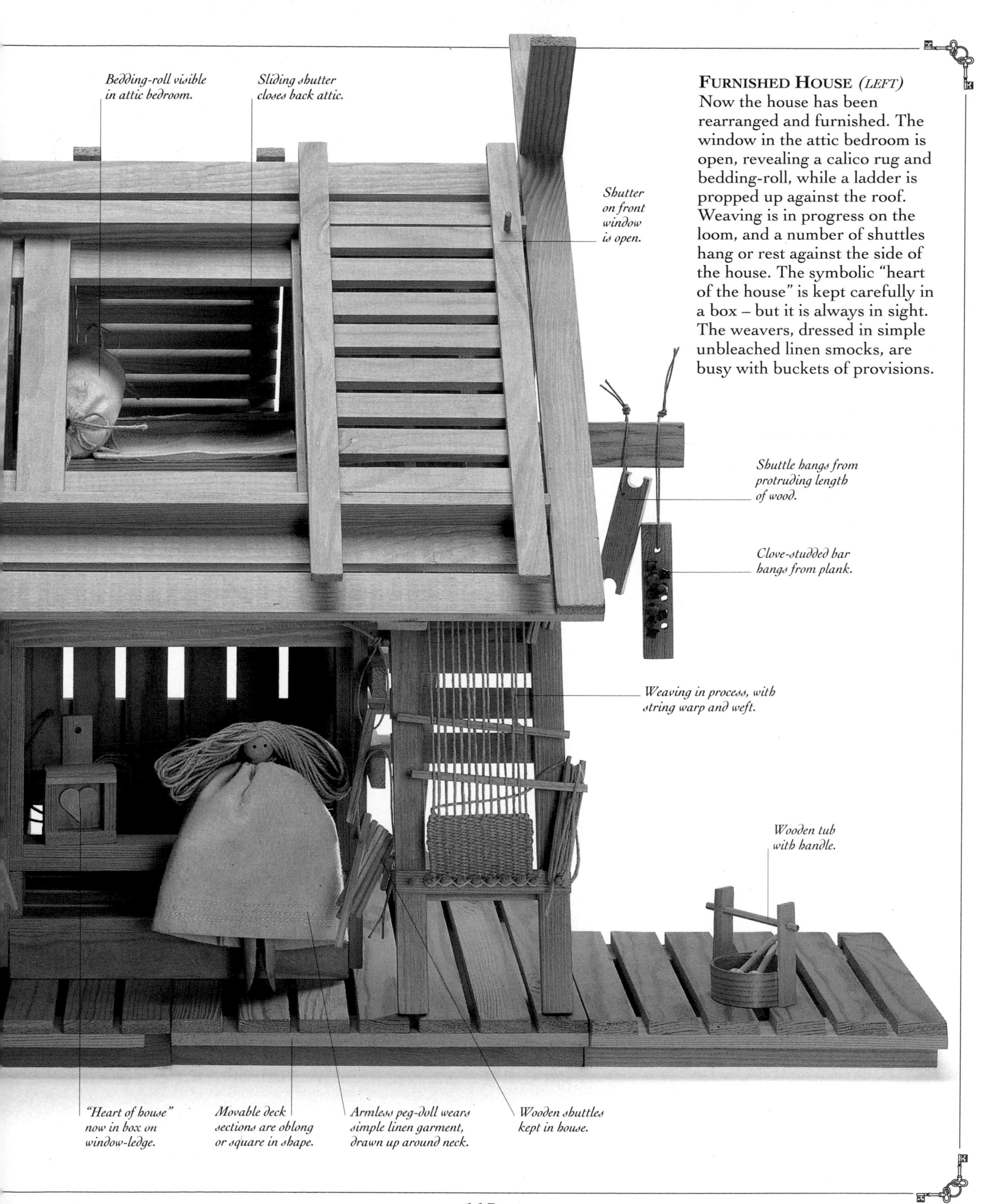
Bedding-roll visible in attic bedroom.
Sliding shutter closes back attic.
Shutter on front window is open.
Shuttle hangs from protruding length of wood.
Clove-studded bar hangs from plank.
Weaving in process, with string warp and weft.
Wooden tub with handle.
"Heart of house" now in box on window-ledge.
Movable deck sections are oblong or square in shape.
Armless peg-doll wears simple linen garment, drawn up around neck.
Wooden shuttles kept in house.

FURNISHED HOUSE *(LEFT)*
Now the house has been rearranged and furnished. The window in the attic bedroom is open, revealing a calico rug and bedding-roll, while a ladder is propped up against the roof. Weaving is in progress on the loom, and a number of shuttles hang or rest against the side of the house. The symbolic "heart of the house" is kept carefully in a box – but it is always in sight. The weavers, dressed in simple unbleached linen smocks, are busy with buckets of provisions.

MOBILE HOMES

German caravan and English houseboat; early 20th century

THESE RATHER UNUSUAL painted mobile homes for dolls were designed as children's playthings. Both are soundly constructed and offer scope for imaginative play, in addition to their basic attraction as pull-along toys.

The caravan, which has a decorative stencilled pattern on the external walls, is of a more complex design than the houseboat; the porch at one end is adorned with flower-boxes, and a drawer beneath the main section provides storage for the wooden porch steps when the caravan is on the move.

The chief ornamentation on the houseboat is the splendid railed deck – albeit with a practical stove pipe pushing through. A rugged, carved wooden Captain stands on deck, contrasting vividly with the two daintily dressed, jointed bisque French dolls who occupy the caravan. The solid metal wheels underneath the houseboat are hidden.

THE FACADE
This enchanting caravan has a pair of green painted wooden shutters at each lace-curtained window; the porch, with its gilded metal balustrade, is supported by wooden pillars.

THE CARAVAN
It seems that no child had the joy of playing with this charming toy: the wallpapers are unmarked, the net curtains and shining "brass" pelmets are immaculate, and the furniture is just as it left the factory – still tied through the painted cardboard floor-covering. White and gold embossed paper decorates the furniture, in the French style.

Painted paper "glazing-bar" stuck to window glass.

Dark blue printed paper "upholstery".

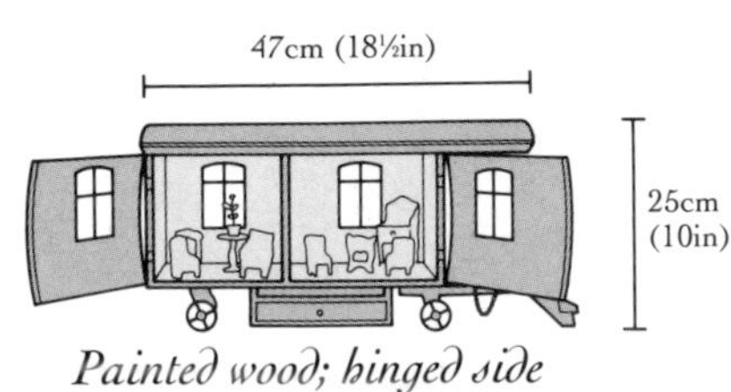

Painted wood; hinged side openings and porch door.

WASHINGTON DOLLS' HOUSE & TOY MUSEUM

Spoked metal wheel on strong wooden axle.

THE HOUSEBOAT

With its distinctive windows, shutters, pierced metal decoration, and original wallpapers in both rooms, this very rare houseboat on wheels is believed to be a 1930s Tri-ang toy.

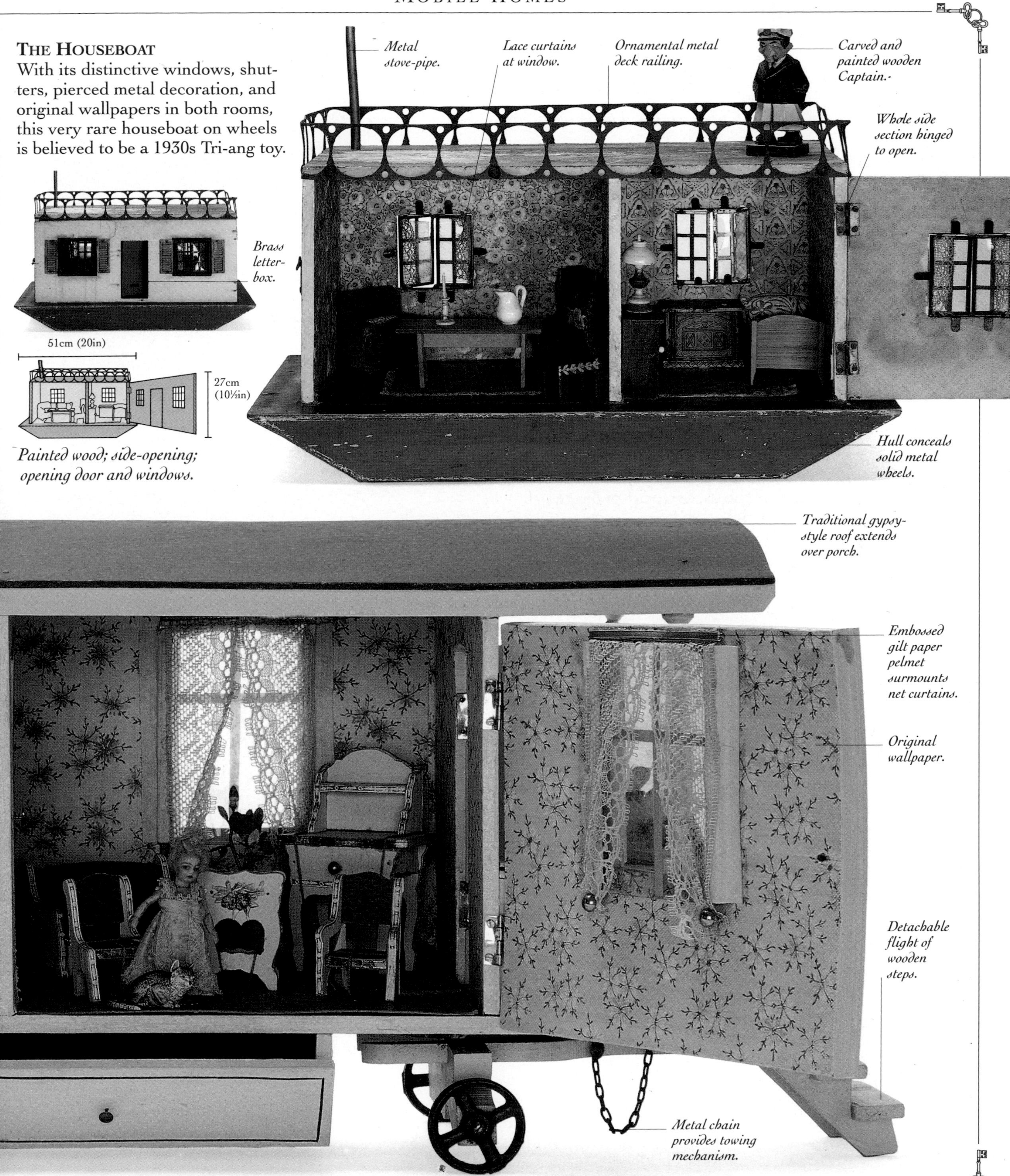

Painted wood; side-opening; opening door and windows.

JAPANESE HOUSE

Japanese dolls' house; shipped to England in 1952

A DOLLS' HOUSE such as this is rare, even in Japan, and it is possible that this was made as a special commission. It is known only that an English photographer who visited Japan in 1952 brought the dolls' house back as a present for his young daughter. Although the house is designed as a dolls' house, it is also an authentic replica of a nineteenth-century Japanese dwelling, with its sliding wooden screens, external bath-house, and room furnishings. Rooms in Japanese houses are measured by the number of mats needed to cover the floors; for example, the upper rooms in this house are six-mat size, whereas the lower room is eight-mat size. Like the mats, the interior and exterior screens are perfect replicas and slide along grooves in the floors and ceilings.

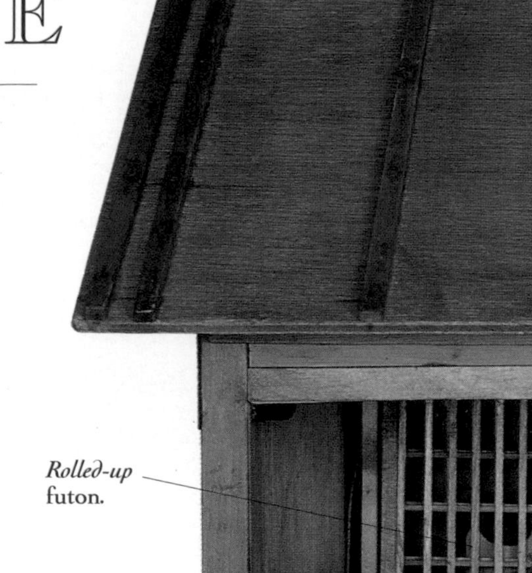

Rolled-up futon.

Paper sunshade.

Kitchen, behind fixed screen on platform, has sliding doors to living area.

FIRST FLOOR

The room on the left has a cupboard with sliding slatted screens, behind which *futons* are stored. The other room, with a shrine in the alcove, is an important guest room; such a room is found in all traditional Japanese homes.

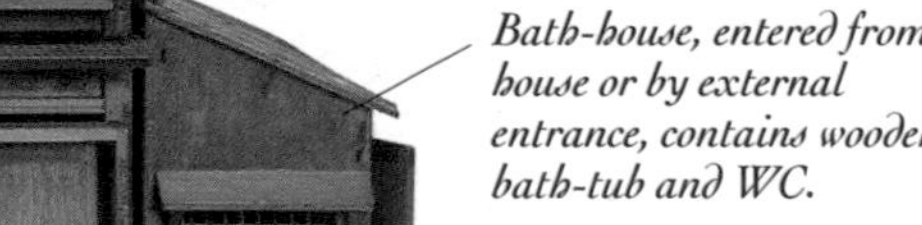

Bath-house, entered from house or by external entrance, contains wooden bath-tub and WC.

Hinged door to bath-house.

Closet for storing external screens when not in use.

Projecting porch protects main entrance to house.

THE FACADE

This house, of natural wood, has no glazed windows; ventilation, protection from the elements, and light is provided by screens. Heavier screens are kept in a closet on the veranda.

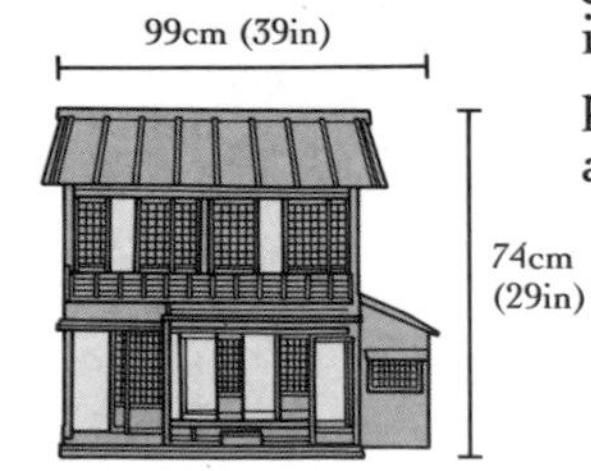

Natural wood; screens slide back or can be removed.

GROUND FLOOR

Silver-papered wooden screens divide the house's largest room from the staircase, vestibule, and external bath-house *(right)*. Similar screens divide the kitchen from the living area.

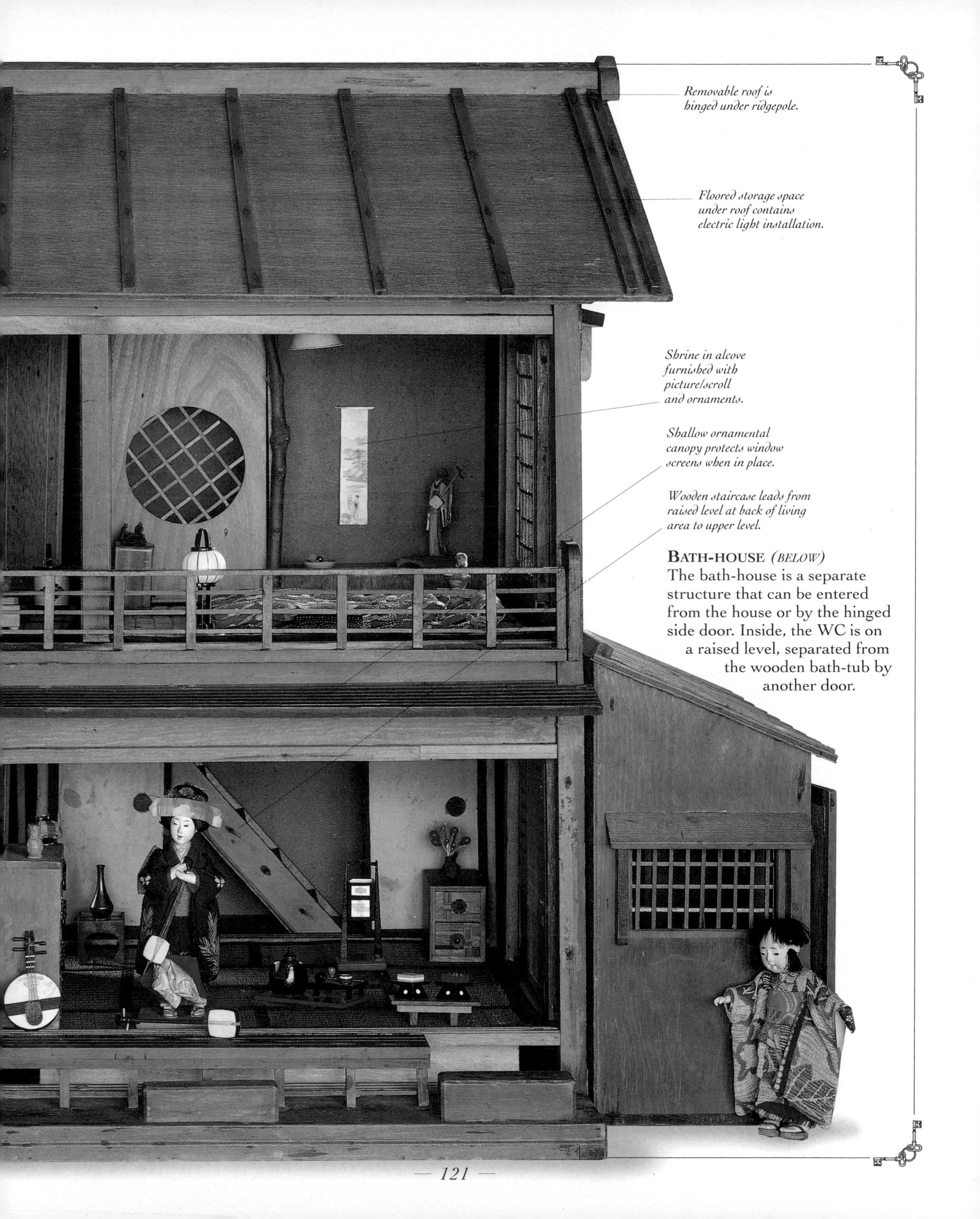
Removable roof is hinged under ridgepole.
Floored storage space under roof contains electric light installation.
Shrine in alcove furnished with picture/scroll and ornaments.
Shallow ornamental canopy protects window screens when in place.
Wooden staircase leads from raised level at back of living area to upper level.

BATH-HOUSE *(BELOW)*
The bath-house is a separate structure that can be entered from the house or by the hinged side door. Inside, the WC is on a raised level, separated from the wooden bath-tub by another door.

JAPANESE STYLE

JAPANESE FURNISHINGS are often stored when not in use, leaving rooms uncluttered. Using *futons* instead of beds, for example, means that sleeping areas are quickly converted into living-rooms. Paper lanterns light the rooms and a few carefully selected ornaments, flowers, and paintings are displayed. The sparse ornamentation and plain walls contribute to the serene effect of Japanese homes. Black or red lacquered items decorated with gold, such as the two small boxes shown here, are particularly prized possessions.

SIX-MAT ROOM *(RIGHT)*
In Japan, straw and string mats bound with black linen are always laid in a traditional pattern. Placed on the mats are three antique stringed instruments, two tiny black lacquered boxes (for writing equipment and a fan), a lamp on a red lacquered base, and a blue-covered bedding-roll *(futon)*; the two low tables hold food and ornaments.

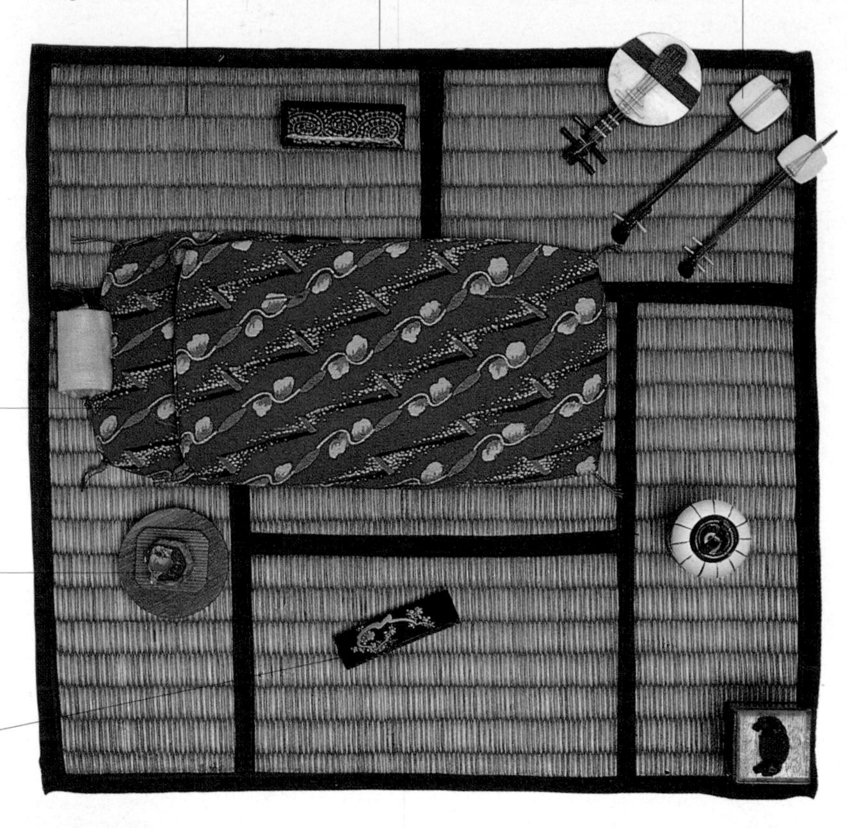

Floor mats made of string and straw.

Each mat bound with black linen.

Samisen – *long, three-stringed Japanese instrument played with plectrum.*

Bedding-roll and pillow stored in cupboard when not in use.

Flower arrangement placed on small table.

Black lacquered box with gold motif on lid.

KITCHEN *(LEFT)*
The cooking-area is on the lower level, while the raised section provides storage space. The sink is piled high with vegetables, and on the green table are a wooden tray and bowls. The wooden mat is a hygienic floor covering.

Child enters kitchen from vestibule level.

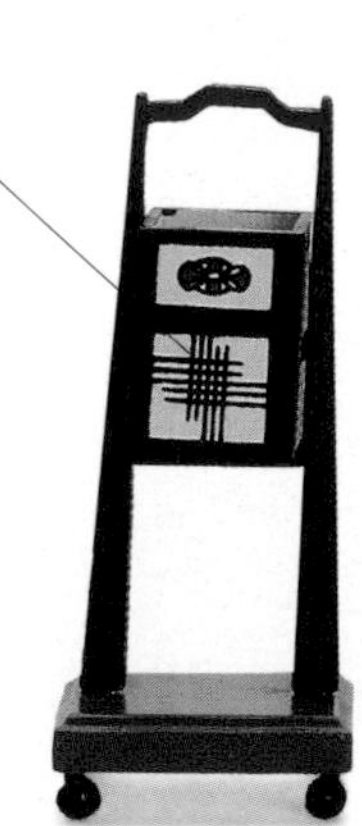

Black lacquer lantern with paper shade.

Floor lantern set on red lacquer platform.

LANTERNS AND TEA THINGS
(RIGHT/BELOW) Candles or oil lamps light these decorative paper lanterns. Equipment for the ritual Japanese tea-ceremony includes a fire-pot and water-dipper. The multi-coloured festival cakes, shown here on their special stands, are made for the Girls' Festival, which is held annually in March.

Festival cake.

Fire-pot on red lacquer tray.

WOODEN CHESTS *(RIGHT)* Like the house itself, these chests are made of natural wood, with simple uncluttered lines. The chest of drawers is beautifully made from different kinds of wood, arranged in patterns.

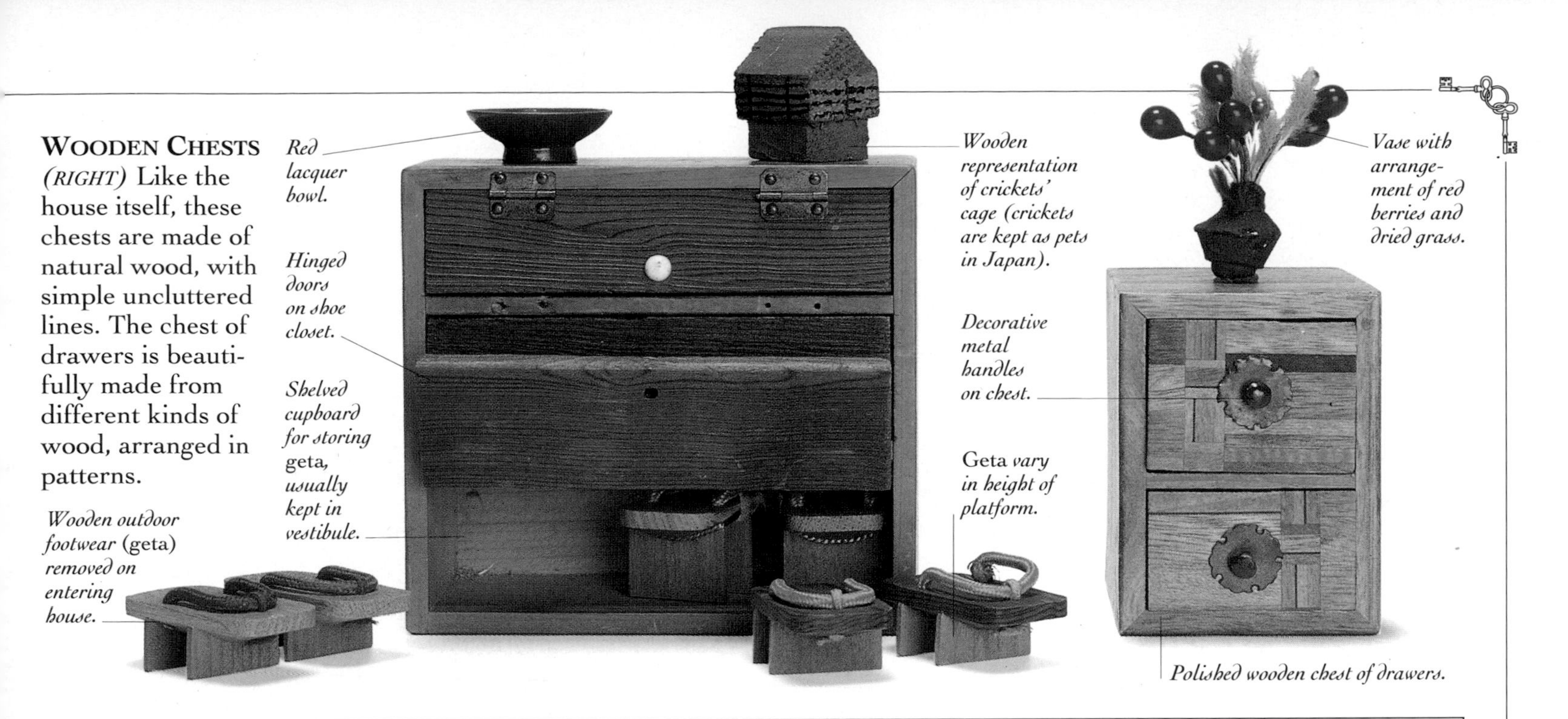

ANTIQUE JAPANESE DOLLS

THESE ANTIQUE DOLLS, who have occupied the dolls' house since it arrived in England from Japan in 1952, came from a collection made by several generations of an English family who lived in Japan for many years. The dolls' heads are covered with a composition of pulverized oyster shells and glue, polished to resemble ivory, while their painted, moulded hands fit on to the wired arms. The dolls, who are fixed in position on wooden stands, have tiny, inset glass eyes, and wigs, both simple and elaborate, that are correctly styled for each character. The intricately detailed costumes, worn by both men and women, include brocaded outer robes *(kimonos)*, traditional sashes *(obis)*, and padded silk undergarments.

TIBETAN HOUSE

— Made in India by Lamaist monks in 1991 —

THIS DOLLS' HOUSE is a representation of a traditional Tibetan house, made in India by monks from the Drepung Loseling monastery who were exiled with the Dalai Lama in 1959. In 1983 the monks resumed their traditional artistic skills and began making dolls and dolls' houses – partly to train new monks and partly to provide an income. This example is made of painted wood in the traditional Tibetan style, with gaily coloured prayer flags flying from the two front corners. The monks blessed the house before packing and sending it off.

THE FACADE
The white facade, with brightly painted door and windows, is typical of a traditional Tibetan house. Each window has an external fabric blind, finished with a white, pleated pelmet.

FIRST FLOOR
The Shrine Room *(right)* has an ornate, symbolically patterned ceiling, shrine, and wall-hanging, while the room on the left contains a colourful prayer table and simple wooden bed.

Incense jar fixed to balcony ledge.

Colourful prayer flags.

Sun-blind pulls out from window-frame.

Base painted to represent bricks.

Hinged double doors painted red and green with large round ornamental handles.

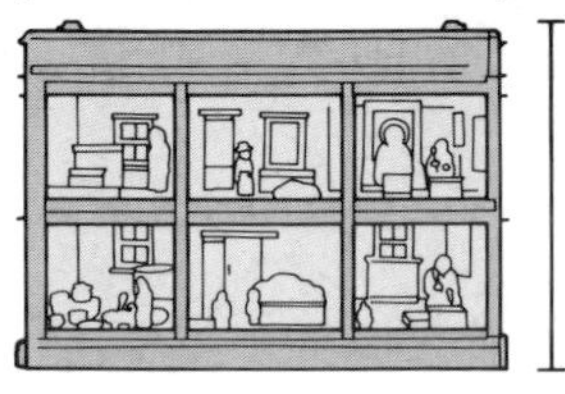

Wooden structure; back-opening; hinged doors.

GROUND FLOOR
A large copper pot for storing grain dominates the kitchen *(left)*, while the middle room is furnished with a lacquered wooden sofa-bed. A carved male figure is seen at prayer in the room on the right.

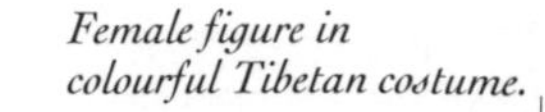

Female figure in colourful Tibetan costume.

Each window has four glazed panes.

Hinged door opens onto front balcony.

Internal window-frame painted lighter shade of blue than exterior frame.

One of eight opening side windows.

Wooden beam-ends painted to match exterior window-frames.

Sliding door into entrance hall.

Walls painted pale green.

Power socket for house's lighting.

TIBETAN TRADITION

ALL THE FURNITURE made by the monks to furnish the Tibetan house is wooden; some pieces are painted but left unadorned, while others are profusely decorated with traditional Tibetan designs. The style of painting varies from the simple suggestion of lacquered work on the sofa-bed in the middle room downstairs, to the fine miniature painting of "Shakyamuni the Gotama" on the tanka in the Shrine Room. Other examples of Tibetan folk art decorate the shrine and prayer-tables and the symbolically patterned ceiling in the Shrine Room. The sofa-bed upstairs is the only undecorated piece, apart from the contents of the kitchen, which include plain ceramic, wood, metal, and plaster items.

WALL-HANGING

(RIGHT) This hand-painted panel shows the deity Shakyamuni, founder of Buddhism in India *c.*500BC. Surrounded by symbols, with the halo of enlightenment above his head, he sits in the lotus position. In his left hand is a monk's begging-bowl; the right invokes the Earth's witness.

Shakyamuni represented with golden body and blue hair.

Deity sits on disc of sun and moon on lotus blossom.

Painting mounted on dark blue fabric backing.

Black ceramic Tibetan mastiff.

Lhasa Apso, of white ceramic.

TIBETAN DOGS *(LEFT)*

The dogs are painted ceramic. The larger, a Tibetan mastiff, is a watch-dog, usually on guard outside the front door. The small dog is a Lhasa Apso, a popular breed in Tibet long before it was seen in the West.

Glazed cooking-pot with removable lid.

Shell decoration on square black cooking stove.

Long metal ladle with hooked handle.

Unglazed mixing bowl for kitchen use.

Ornately decorated hand-painted shrine.

Traditional Tibetan colours and patterns.

SHRINE AND SOFA BED

(LEFT/BELOW) The shrine is painted in a popular Tibetan colour scheme of red, yellow, and gold. A traditionally patterned mattress or bed-board rests on the sofa-bed.

Imitation lacquer decoration.

COOKING EQUIPMENT

(ABOVE) The well-equipped kitchen has pots, pans, jars, and a set of unglazed pottery bowls. A large ceramic pot sits on the stove, which is fuelled by dried yak's dung.

TIBETAN CHARACTERS

LIKE THE HOUSE and its contents, the dolls were carved by more than one craftsman, so each interpretation is unique, even though the proportions and characters for all the figures had been agreed upon. As scale was held to be of little importance, the dolls vary in size from 8–15cm (3–6in) in height. Even if the figures were individually carved, it appears that all the faces, and possibly the costumes, were painted by the same artist. There is certainly a family likeness, though each doll has a definite personal identity. Predictably, the monk's face is unlined and serene, unlike those of his two relatives who are praying with him.

PRAYING FIGURES *(BELOW)*
The monk of the family is joined by two relatives, each of whom holds a *mala* (Tibetan Buddhist rosary) and a prayer-wheel.

Serene expression is well painted on realistic face.

Monk praying at decorated prayer table.

Prayer-wheel revolves to spin prayers within.

Detailed facial expression with lines on forehead and face.

Wooden hand pierced to hold prayer-beads.

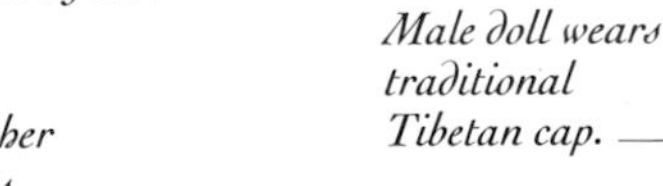

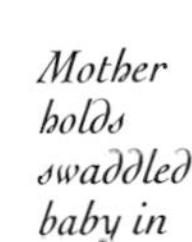

Tibetan Buddhist rosary of strung "pearl" beads.

Monk sits on plain wooden bed-board.

Multi-coloured apron is part of regional Tibetan costume.

Prayer table always placed by bed.

STANDING FIGURES *(BELOW)*
The dolls are beautifully carved and painted, with their colourful costumes designed to represent people from many regions of Tibet. The men wear colourful, traditional Tibetan padded boots.

Regional variation of basic Tibetan man's costume.

Costume has decorative gold-painted pattern.

Crown of hat is braided.

Mother holds swaddled baby in arms.

Male doll wears traditional Tibetan cap.

GUYANESE HOUSE

Made by Guyanese student Ruth Bollers in 1992

RUTH BOLLERS, A GUYANESE student living in London, based this dolls' house on her childhood home, which she had recently revisited. Having always been interested in craftwork, Ruth chose toy-making for her diploma work at the London College of Furniture. She created this dolls' house as a toy, but was determined that it should accurately portray an aspect of Guyanese culture.

The house represents the type of dwelling found in Georgetown – the capital of Guyana – or in any similarly flat area of the country where flooding is frequent. Houses in such areas have structures of greenheart or purpleheart wood, with walls and floors of varnished pine or mahogany. Their furniture is usually made of pine, mahogany, cane, or a mixture of local woods whose colouring creates a toning effect.

The dolls' house contains essential items found in any Guyanese home – a hammock slung in the shade under the house, a mosquito net over the bed, and a rocking-chair on the veranda, as well as a stove, tables, and chairs. Since Ruth made this house for my collection in 1992, I have added dolls and a basic shower and WC, all made by Ruth to an appropriate design.

Wooden staircase provides access to front veranda.

Hinged door opens into room.

Verandas at front and rear of house provide extra living space.

Colour-stained wooden chairs and settee.

Multi-coloured woven rug with fringed ends.

Windows positioned to provide maximum ventilation.

Kitchen sink and stove of natural wood with silver-painted details.

Non-toxic wood dyes used to colour furniture.

Staircase gives access to veranda at rear of house.

OVERHEAD VIEW
The simple wooden furniture in the house was designed for young children.

SIDE VIEW *(RIGHT)*
The sloping roof, the stilts that raise the house, the outside staircases, and the verandas, are all typical features of a Guyanese house. As the house was designed as a plaything, the windows were left unglazed.

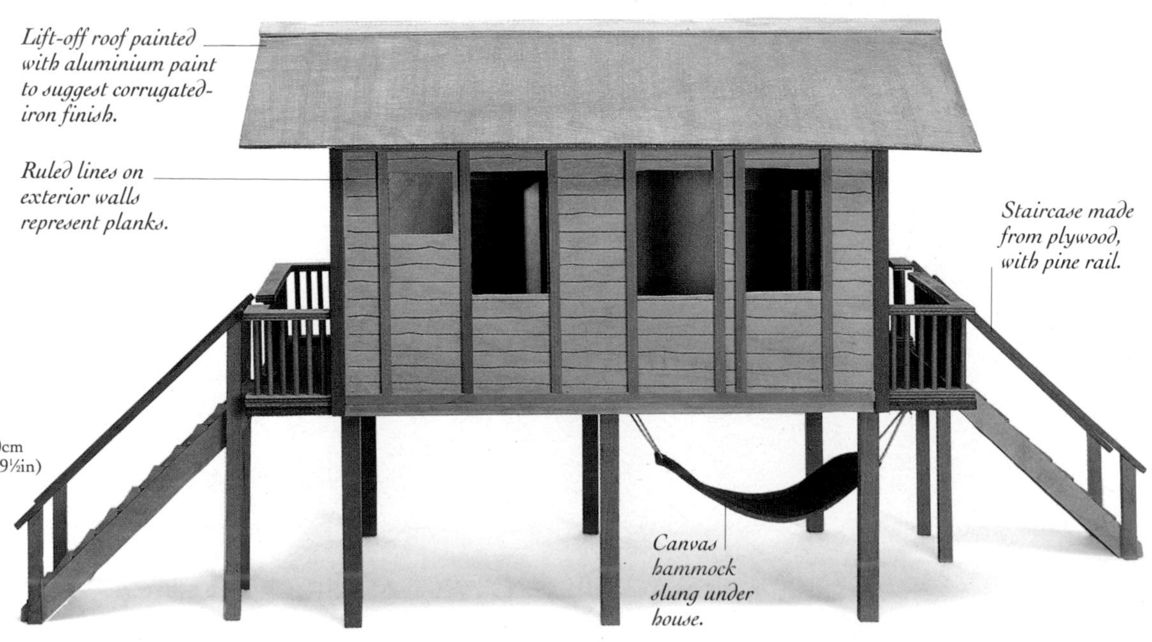

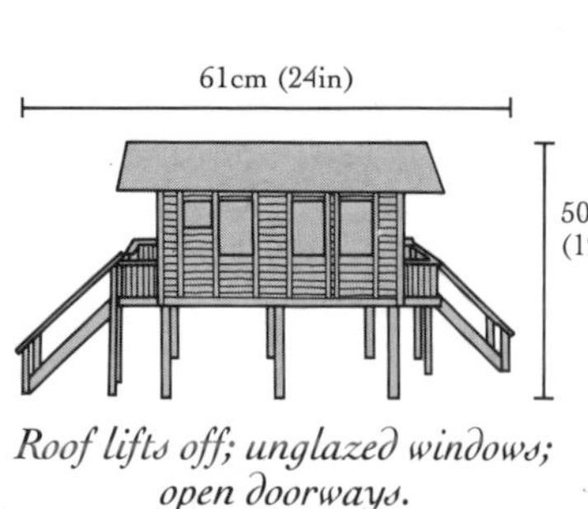

Roof lifts off; unglazed windows; open doorways.

FRONT VIEW
This simple house displays many features essential for comfort in the hot, wet climate of Guyana. Verandas at each end provide cool areas for both relaxation and work, such as sewing and even cooking. A mosquito net is visible through the window.

Roof lifts off to give access to interior.

Mosquito net hung over bed provides essential protection.

Walls of house made of birch plywood.

Open railings on verandas provide extra ventilation.

Stilts of sturdy pine support house above flood level.

White-painted rocking-chair on veranda.

Doll has simple painted features.

Arms, made of slivers of wood, are jointed to bodies with string.

Dolls made of turned and carved mahogany.

THE DOLLS
(RIGHT) Like the house and its contents, these simple dolls are designed as playthings. Their painted, varnished costumes are typical of everyday Guyanese clothing: the man wears a white singlet and black trousers, and his partner wears a colourful sari.

CONTAINER HOUSES

Miniature houses with a practical purpose

FOR CENTURIES, houses have provided inspiration for the design of containers. House-shaped sewing-boxes, made from ivory or bone, were popular in Britain in the nineteenth century (Chinese straw-work boxes with removable roofs/lids are a modern version). Fragrant pastille-burners and ceramic night-light holders, in the guise of cottages, houses, and even of castles, were popular with the Victorians, whereas musical boxes, housed in miniature Swiss chalets, are long-standing favourites. House-shaped collecting- and money-boxes are practical adaptations, while other dual-purpose containers include lunch-boxes and handbags for children. Most container houses, however, are colourfully printed tins and cardboard boxes, which are often filled with edible goods or items such as china or writing-paper.

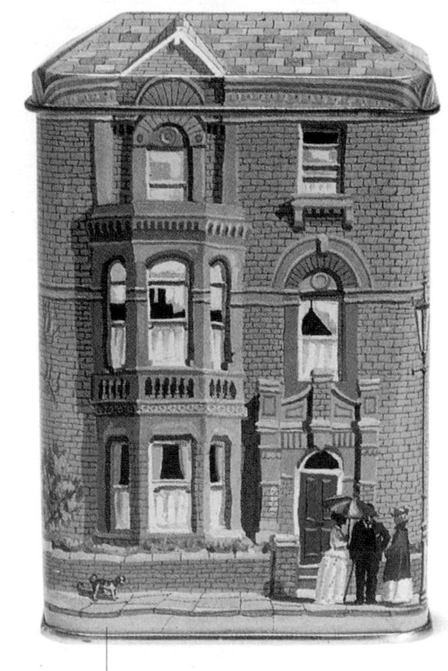

Printed tin with different design on each side.

HOUSE TIN *(ABOVE)* Decorative house-shaped tins range from small, flat pill-boxes to tall house shapes, of the type shown above. They are usually made with removable or hinged lids, representing the roofs of the buildings.

STRAW-WORK BOX *(BELOW)* This well-constructed model represents the Capitol building in Washington, D.C. Chinese straw-work boxes, which are rapidly becoming collectors' items, are usually small and colourful oriental-style houses.

Top section lifts off to reveal padded space in base.

Straw pillars adorn facade.

Slit for coins to be dropped into house.

Painted papier mâché collecting-box.

Stuck-on printed paper window.

COLLECTING-BOX *(ABOVE)* Miniature houses make ideal collecting and money-boxes. Dr Barnardo's Homes (now known as Barnardo's) used boxes like the one shown here until 1971.

SWISS MUSICAL BOX *(BELOW)* Musical boxes have always been one of Switzerland's most popular souvenirs. This carved and painted wooden example dates from the 1930s.

Hinged roof allows access to musical mechanism.

Base raised on four legs.

Winding-key fixed under base.

THE PRACTICALITIES

If the dolls' houses in this book have inspired you to start your own collection, this practical section will give you first-hand advice on where to start and what to look for, as well as tips on identifying miniatures. The hints on conservation and restoration will be useful if you already own a dolls' house, or plan to acquire an old one.

• GOTTSCHALK HOUSE •
This c.1900–1910 German example illustrates a number of problems likely to be found on old dolls' houses.

COLLECTING DOLLS' HOUSES

DOLLS' HOUSE HUNTING is now easier, though more costly, than it was a few decades ago. It is no longer thought odd for adults to buy miniature houses for themselves as well as for children: in Europe and in the United States, collectors' clubs and magazines flourish and "For Sale" advertisements are commonplace. If you are a prospective buyer, you can look for a house at auctions, specialist shops, or at toy and dolls' house fairs; and if you want a really special house, you can commission a craftsman to design and build one to your individual requirements.

TEACHING TOYS *(RIGHT) Dolls' houses have always been popular gifts for little girls. Mothers, regarding them as educational toys, fondly hoped the child would learn the principles of good housekeeping as she played.*

— PRELIMINARY RESEARCH —

Whatever type of house you decide on, it is usually helpful to do some research first. If you are particularly interested in antique dolls' houses, libraries and book shops now stock a splendid selection of well-illustrated books, many of which have been written by specialists on the subject.

Museums, of course, are immensely useful for research and provide an opportunity to view for yourself some of the houses you may have already seen illustrated in books; they may also enable you to see the size of a particular dolls' house, which can be an important consideration if space is limited.

Unless you have already found your "dream house" in a shop, an auction house is probably the next place to visit. Most have items on view for a day or so before sales (dates are advertised in newspapers and magazines), and catalogues are available. But do inspect everything carefully; however charming a dolls' house may be, if it is affected by dry rot or woodworm it will need

AUCTION HOUSE *(LEFT) In front of the rostrum at Christie's auction house in London, Olivia Bristol, their doll and dolls' house expert, views two items from a forthcoming sale. Auction-house staff offer specialist advice and valuations on request.*

ANNUAL FAIR *(RIGHT) Dolls' house and miniature fairs are held regularly in many countries. The stall of dolls' house maker Peter Mattinson at the London Dolls' House Festival, an annual event, is shown here.*

MASTER MINIATURIST
(LEFT) Leading miniaturist John Hodgson creates exquisite furniture as well as miniature buildings to house them. Some, including this Georgian house, are on display at Hever Castle, Kent (see pp.48–51).

DOLLS' HOUSE MUSEUM
(RIGHT) Privately owned museums are especially useful when the owner's knowledge is reflected in carefully selected exhibitions. Flora Gill Jacobs displays a fascinating collection of dolls' houses and rooms at her museum in Washington, D.C.

careful thought before purchase – and thoughtful care afterwards. Dolls' house fairs are also worth visiting; most have stalls selling houses, furnishings, and accessories, both old and new. The bigger fairs attract sellers from home and abroad, so the range of goods on sale is often extensive.

Another advantage of attending a fair is the opportunity it provides to talk to dolls' house makers. Many of these craftsmen and women hire stalls to display their houses, and they are always willing to discuss building plans with prospective customers. They also supply the specialist dolls' house shops which, although virtually unknown 25 years ago, now offer an indispensable service to enthusiasts and collectors.

— KITS AND CUSTOMIZED HOUSES —

Specialist shops also supply the books and kits you need if you decide to make your own dolls' house; the shop's owner will be happy to offer advice, or to recommend professional dolls' house makers who design and build to commission.

The high cost of antique and custom-made dolls' houses has encouraged many people to buy dolls' houses that were designed originally as children's playthings, and to adapt them to their own requirements. This is one way of having an exclusive dolls' house although, obviously, it will not really compete with the professionally made ones in the recognized 1:12 collector's scale. Custom-made houses will have more realistically proportioned rooms and staircases, for example, and may reflect a particular house-style, or even replicate one particular building in miniature.

Another option, if funds are limited, is to make a house from a standard kit, and then to embellish the basic building with your own individual touches. For example, you can produce authentic, miniature replicas of photographs from a family album by reducing the full-scale originals to the required size on a photocopying machine. The creative possibilities are endless – and are all part of the fascination for the dolls' house enthusiast.

LONDON DOLLS' HOUSE SHOP *(ABOVE)*
Shops specializing in dolls' houses and miniatures are invaluable to collectors trying to track down individual items. Michal Morse has catered for both collectors and children since opening Britain's first specialist shop, The Dolls' House, in London in 1971.

DOCUMENTING MINIATURES

IN ADDITION TO the sheer pleasure that they find in miniatures and dolls' houses, collectors and enthusiasts have another, more academic interest in the subject. One aspect of this arises from the function of miniatures and dolls' houses as historical records, providing social historians and other researchers with valuable information about life-styles, architecture, and interior decoration from particular periods of history, in different parts of the world.

This is most obvious in the case of antique dolls' houses. Some splendid examples, like the baby house at Nostell Priory, do resemble the mansions in which they are still displayed; a few, such as the *c.*1740 King's Lynn baby house, are exact replicas of their original owners' homes.

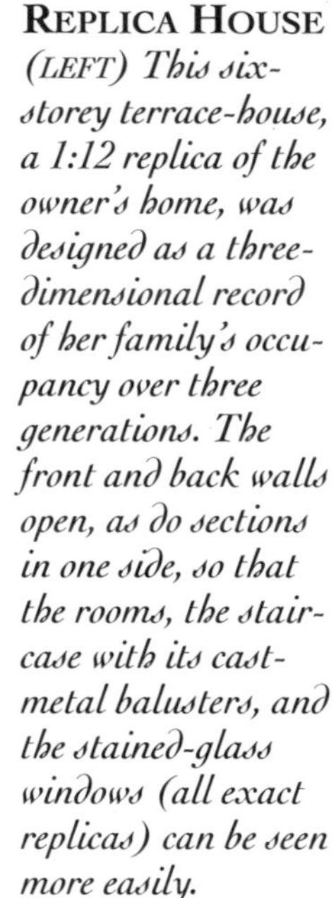

REPLICA HOUSE *(LEFT) This six-storey terrace-house, a 1:12 replica of the owner's home, was designed as a three-dimensional record of her family's occupancy over three generations. The front and back walls open, as do sections in one side, so that the rooms, the staircase with its cast-metal balusters, and the stained-glass windows (all exact replicas) can be seen more easily.*

— ORIGINAL RECORDS —

It sometimes happens, though sadly all too seldom, that the provenance of a dolls' house has been recorded and kept with it: Uppark's baby house is one very well-known English example. In Holland, Sara Ploos van Amstel kept meticulously detailed notebooks, which relate to the making and furnishing of her two famous cabinet houses *(see pp.34–37)*, and these are the most satisfying references that any researcher could desire.

Collectors today are aware that even modern, twentieth-century dolls' houses will become valuable research material for historians in the future, especially if both the interiors and facades of the houses are authentic replicas. With this in mind, some set out to reconstruct, in miniature, their own homes and life-styles, or other examples from contemporary society. Such a project could prove

AVERY CHAIR *(LEFT/ABOVE)*
The English needle manufacturer, W. Avery & Son of Redditch, Worcestershire, started making metal needlecases shaped like pieces of furniture in the 1860s. Their clearly stamped pieces are a joy to researchers.

CALLCOTT LABEL *(RIGHT)*
This label, which almost covers the base of a small papier mâché house, made in 1914 (see pp.72–73), *identifies the latter as a commercially made British product.*

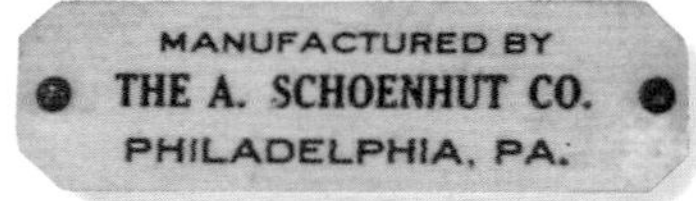

SCHOENHUT LABEL *(RIGHT) Although it is fairly easy to recognize a Schoenhut dolls' house, a label is always a bonus.*

BLISS LABEL *(RIGHT)*
The name on many Bliss houses is incorporated into the chromo-lithographed design of the facade, as on the example shown here (see pp.90–91).

expensive if the fixtures and fittings as well as the house are made to order. It is possible to chronicle family or local history on a more modest scale, however, by commissioning, or even making, a cardboard or moulded plaster model, with accurately painted details. Even such simplified records merit labels of some kind; it is important, not only to the creators of modern miniature replicas, but to future researchers also, that the maker's name and the date and address of the full-scale house should be documented in or on the miniature version. For a house to be regarded as an authentic historical record, this is essential.

— THE IMPORTANCE OF LABELS —

This brings us to another area of great interest to collectors: that of identifying and authenticating dolls' houses, dolls, and dolls' house furniture, and the difficulty of doing so without the aid of labels or records. Certainly, collectors and researchers bless those manufacturers whose names can be found on their products. Whether they use fixed labels, or employ designs with the name incorporated into a pattern, firms such as Bliss and Schoenhut deserve praise and gratitude.

Most infuriating and regrettable are the omissions of those artist-craftsmen and other small firms whose products were sold without any identifying marks. One craftswoman, Florence Callcott, has added greatly to the interest of her creations with her illustrated label, which is almost as big as the base of her little house *(see above)*. On the other hand, the 1930s handcrafted Westacre Village "lacquered" dolls' house furniture, and the tin pieces produced by a well-established firm, Evans & Cartwright, in the early nineteenth century, have only recently been identified after researchers' painstaking efforts.

In the absence of trademarks, collectors have to rely on their knowledge and experience when attempting to identify or authenticate a piece – knowledge gathered from extensive reading, visits to museums, talking to other collectors, and the on-going research that provides so much interest for those involved in the world of miniatures.

BLISS FURNITURE *(LEFT)*
Though best known for their dolls' houses, the American firm Bliss of Pawtucket also made sets of furniture. One c.1901 Bliss line had pieces decorated with letters of the alphabet. There were several sets, mainly parlour and bedroom furniture, with different designs and colours. Although each piece had letters, usually printed in brown or red, the surrounding decoration varied from a simple scroll to a complicated design incorporating children's figures.

RESTORATION AND CONSERVATION

IT IS SOMETIMES difficult to decide how, or even if, an antique dolls' house should be restored. Pending expert advice, a good rule is "when in doubt, do nothing". Often, more damage is done by over-restoration than by the ravages of time, reducing both the historical interest and the monetary value of the house in question.

However, if an antique dolls' house has been over-painted, papered with modern wallpapers, and given synthetic curtains, these should be removed and, if possible, old papers and fabrics used instead. You can sometimes find old worn shawls, clothing, and odd ends of wallpapers in junk shops or at jumble sales; old work-baskets may contain scraps of antique fabric, braid, or lace that may also prove useful.

Woodworm and dry rot must be treated immediately. Such problems, along with any damage to woodwork, or corroded or rusted metalwork, require expert advice, and possibly professional treatment, before any restoration work is attempted.

Whether to install electric lighting is a personal choice, but in general it is not advisable if the dolls' house was made before such lighting would have featured in a similar, full-scale house.

Careful conservation, including keeping dolls' houses away from direct heat, light, or damp, and regular housekeeping, will ensure their well-being and minimize any future restoration problem.

Peeling wallpaper.
Graffiti on wallpaper can be hidden by furniture if not removable.
Replacement glass required for window.
Vertical break in facade needs repair.
Modern wrapping-paper used to paper this room.
Damage to "stonework" can be filled in.
Slight water-stain on brick-effect base paper.

MUSEUM CONSERVATOR
(ABOVE) Ella Hendricks, conservator at the Frans Hals Museum in Haarlem, Holland, is shown at work on one of the outer doors of Sara Ploos van Amstel's cabinet house (see pp.34–37).

BLISS HOUSE WINDOW
(RIGHT) The painted window on the ground floor of this otherwise delightful small Bliss house is neither the original nor a correct replica. Someone has reproduced the design of the painted upper windows, but research would have shown that this window was originally glazed. Glass should replace the painted window to restore the house to its original appearance.

DAMAGED DOLLS' HOUSE
(LEFT) Conservation alone is not enough for this Gottschalk house, but, with replica replacement doors and windows, repairs to the facade, and the removal of modern wallpapers and overpainting on the roof, door, and facade interior, it may again become a desirable residence.

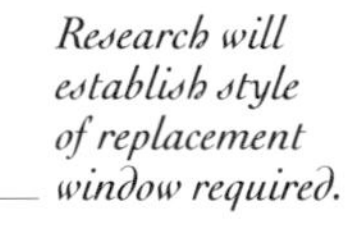
Roof has been over-painted.
Mended facade requires new hinges, fitted in original positions.
Door over-painted.
Research will establish style of replacement window required.
Metal balcony needs conservation rather than restoration.

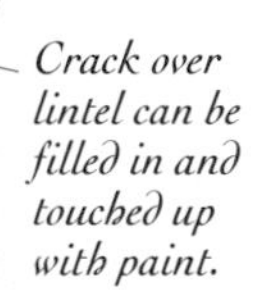
Crack over lintel can be filled in and touched up with paint.
Authentic replacement for missing door required.
Wrinkled floor-paper; not original.

EXTERIOR PROBLEMS

UNRESTORED ORIGINAL
(ABOVE) Opinions vary on how much active repairing is acceptable. In this case the owner chose to retain the original, damaged paintwork, rather than to paint over the missing section.

MISSING DOOR *(ABOVE)*
In this example, the missing door severely affects the look of the dolls' house, and it would be reasonable to replace it with a replica copied from the door on an identical model.

LOST FACADE DETAIL
(ABOVE) The missing quoining on the corner will not hasten the deterioration of this dolls' house; whether it should be replaced is, therefore, a matter of personal opinion about conservation.

DAMAGED ROOF *(ABOVE)*
The deterioration on the roof of this Schoenhut bungalow may become worse and, if the corner is knocked, the damage could be serious. Restoration now appears to be the sensible option.

INTERIOR PROBLEMS

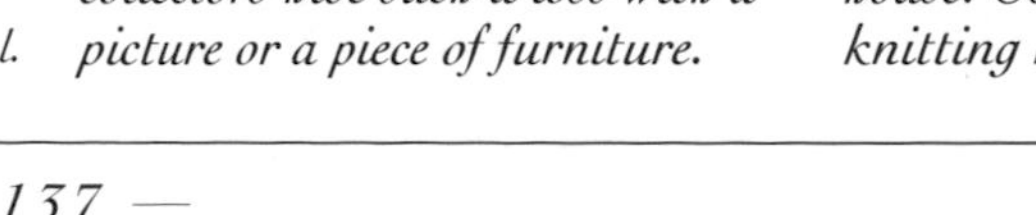

TORN WALLPAPER *(ABOVE)*
It is unlikely that you will find a matching piece to replace torn or missing wallpaper, and replicas are usually unconvincing. Many collectors hide such a loss with a picture or a piece of furniture.

REPLACEMENT CURTAINS
(ABOVE) Pieces from an old paisley shawl, or scraps of old fabrics, will provide excellent curtains for an antique dolls' house. Use old wooden or bone knitting needles for curtain-rods.

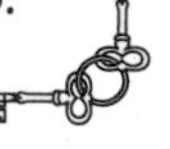

ADDRESSES

CANADA

DAISY DOLLHOUSE
P.O. Box 92
Flatbush, Alta, TOG OZO

THE DOLL ATTIC & CO.
62 Brock Street
Kingston, Ont., K7L 1R9

THE LITTLE DOLLHOUSE CO.
617 Mt. Pleasant Road
Toronto, Ont., M4S 2M5

ROSS' TREASURE HOUSE LTD
823 1st Street West
North Vancouver
B.C. V7P 1A4

DENMARK

LEGOLAND PARK
Nordmarksvej 9
DK-7190 Billund

FRANCE

MUSEE DES ARTS DECORATIFS
Départment Jouets
Palais du Louvre
107 rue de Rivoli
75001 Paris

MUSEE HISTORIC DU JOUET
2 Enclos de L'Arbayr
78300 Poissy

GERMANY

BAYERN STADTMUSEUM
Postfach 80331
München

GERMANISCHES NATIONALMUSEUM
Kornmarkt 1
8500 Nürnberg

SPIELZEUGMUSEUM
Karlstrasse 13
8500 Nürnberg

HOLLAND

CENTRAAL MUSEUM
Agnietenstraat 1
NL 3500, GC Utrecht

FRANS HALSMUSEUM
P.O. Box 3365
2001 DJ Haarlem

GEMEENTEMUSEUM
Stadhouderslaan 41
25178V The Hague

RIJKSMUSEUM
P.O. Box 74888
1070 DN Amsterdam

SWEDEN

NORDISKA MUSEET
Djugårdsvägen 6–16
115 93 Stockholm

DRAPERY SHOP *(LEFT)*
Though basically just a cardboard box, whose hinged lid folds forward to form the tiled-effect floor, this type of shop was a popular plaything during the 1930s. Both the dolls – a shop assistant and customer inspecting a bolt of material – are cheap, German, pegged-wooden dolls, c.1920s, wearing original clothes.

SWITZERLAND

HAUS ZUM KIRSCHGARTEN
Elisabethenstrasse 27
CH-4051 Basel

UNITED KINGDOM

BETHNAL GREEN MUSEUM OF CHILDHOOD
Cambridge Heath Road
London E2 9PA

DOLLS' HOUSE MUSEUM
23 High Street
Arundel
W. Sussex BN18 9AD

MUSEUM OF CHILDHOOD
42 High Street
Edinburgh EH1 1TG

MUSEUM OF CHILDHOOD
117 Main Street
Haworth
Keighley
Yorkshire BD22 8DU

MUSEUM OF CHILDHOOD
Church Street
Ribchester
Lancashire PR3 3YE

MUSEUM OF CHILDHOOD
Sudbury Hall
Sudbury
Derbyshire DE6 5HT

POLLOCK'S TOY MUSEUM
1 Scala Street
London W1P 1LT

PRESTON HALL MUSEUM
Yarm Road
Stockton-on-Tees
Cleveland TS18 3RH

TOY & TEDDY MUSEUM
373 Clifton Drive North
Lytham St Anne's
Lancashire FY8 2PA

VIVIEN GREENE COLLECTION
The Rotunda
Grove House
Iffley Turn
Oxford, OX4 4DU
(Private collection; viewing by prior arrangement only; no children under 16)

WARWICK DOLLS' MUSEUM
Oken House
Warwick
Warwickshire CV34 4BP

A WORLD IN MINIATURE
North Pier, Oban
Argyll PA34 5QD

WORTHING MUSEUM
Chapel Road
Worthing
W. Sussex BN11 1HP

USA

ANGEL'S ATTIC
516 Colorado Avenue
Santa Monica
Calif. 90401–2408

MARGARET WOODBURY STRONG MUSEUM
1 Manhattan Square
Rochester, N.Y. 14607

MUSEUM OF THE CITY OF NEW YORK
1220 Fifth Avenue
New York, N.Y. 10029

MUSEUM OF SCIENCE AND INDUSTRY
5700 Lakeshore Drive
Chicago, Ill. 60637

SMITHSONIAN INSTITUTION
Museum of American History
Washington, D.C. 20560

TOY & MINIATURE MUSEUM
5235 Oak Street
Kansas City, Mo. 64112

WASHINGTON DOLLS' HOUSE & TOY MUSEUM
5236 44th Street N.W.
Washington D.C. 20015

GLOSSARY

ALCOVE Vaulted recess in wall.
ARCHITRAVE Moulding around doorway or window; beam resting on upper part of pillar.
BABY HOUSE English term for miniature house in seventeenth and eighteenth centuries.
BALUSTER Pillar or post supporting hand-rail.
BALUSTRADE Railing supported by row of balusters.
BAROUCHE Four-wheeled horse-drawn carriage.
BAY Projecting window.
BEVEL Angle, other than right angle, between two surfaces.
BIEDERMEIER Style of conventional furniture popular in Germany, 1810–45.
BISQUE Unglazed porcelain.
CABINET HOUSE Cabinet (often Dutch) adapted as miniature house, containing collection of *objets d'art*.
CABRIOLE LEG Type of leg on furniture with upper convex curve tapering to lower concave curve.

CASEMENT WINDOW Vertically hinged window.
CHAFING-DISH Dish with heating device underneath for keeping food warm at table.
CHROMOLITHOGRAPHY Printing technique for producing coloured prints.
CLAVICHORD Keyboard instrument with thin wire strings.
COMPTOIR Room used as office.
CORBEL Stone or timber bracket providing support.
CORNICE Moulding along top of building, or just below ceiling.
CREEL Wickerwork basket.
CUPBOARD HOUSE Cupboard converted to contain miniature, furnished rooms.
DADO Lower part of wall, decorated separately.
DECOUPAGE Surface decorated with shapes or illustrations cut from paper.
DORMER Vertical window, set in sloping roof.
EAVES Area of roof projecting beyond wall.
ENTABLATURE Architrave, frieze, and cornice resting on columns.
ENTRESOL Low storey between ground and first floors.
ESCUTCHEON Metal plate surrounding key-hole.
FAIENCE Decorated porcelain or earthenware.
FASCIA Flat, vertical surface above shop window.
FANLIGHT Semicircular window above door, often with radiating glazing-bars.
FICHU Woman's scarf or shawl of light material, popular in eighteenth century.
FINIAL Decorative addition to top of post or gable.
FLAGSTONES Large stone slabs used for paving.
FONTANGE Towering headdress of ribbon and lace, popular in England in seventeenth century.
FRETWORK Decorative wood carving or open-work.
FRIEZE Horizontal decoration at top of wall.
GABLE Triangular section of wall at end of ridged roof.
GEORGIAN Period in British history *c.*1714–1830; style of architecture and furniture popular in eighteenth century.
GLAZING BARS Wooden bars holding window-panes in position.
HALF-TESTER BED Bed with canopy over head end.
JABOT Ruffle or frill worn at neck of garment.
JARDINIERE Ornamental pot or stand for plants.
KEYSTONE Central stone of arch.
LAPPETS Small flaps of lace hanging from headdress.

BLUE-ROOF HOUSE *(LEFT) Although it looks similar to many lithographed, Bliss-type American houses, this model is German, made c.1900. It is probably from the line of "blue-roof" dolls' houses made from the mid-nineteenth century in Moritz Gottschalk's works in Marienberg, Germany.*

LYING-IN ROOM Room for confinement in childbirth.
OBJET D'ART Small object of artistic merit.
MANSARD ROOF Roof with two slopes on each side, the lower slopes being steeper.
MODILLION Ornamental bracket under cornice.
NICHE Decorative recess in wall.
ORMOLU Gold-coloured alloy.
PALLADIAN Style of architecture characterized by symmetry and harmonious proportions.
PEDIMENT Triangular section above door or window.
PEWTER Alloy containing tin, lead, and sometimes other metals.
PICTURE-RAIL Wood or metal rail from which pictures are hung.
PROVENANCE Proof of place of origin of work of art.
QUOINS Cornerstones.
RISER Flat, vertical section of step or stair.
ROCOCO Elaborate style of architecture and decoration.
SASH WINDOW Window that slides up and down in grooves.
SCONCE Wall bracket holding candles and lights.
SKIRTING-BOARD Wooden section along bottom of wall.
SPLAT Central part of chair back.
STUART Relating to period of British architecture *c.*1603–49.
TERRACOTTA Brownish red, unglazed earthenware.
TETE-A-TETE S-shaped sofa for two people, allowing them to sit almost face to face.
TORCHERE Tall narrow stand holding candelabrum.
TREAD Flat, horizontal section of step or stair.
TROMPE L'OEIL Painting that gives illusion of reality.
TRUG Long, shallow basket for flowers, fruit, or vegetables.
TYMPANUM Triangular space between arch and lintel of doorway, or pediment's cornices.
VICTORIAN Relating to period of British history 1837–1901.
VIRGINAL Small table-top version of harpsichord.
WAINSCOT Lower interior wall section, often panelled in wood.

INDEX

GATEFOLD ENTRIES

Entries from the gatefold section, which falls between pages 12 and 13 of the book, are indicated in the index by the letters "gf".

A

B

C

D

E

F

G

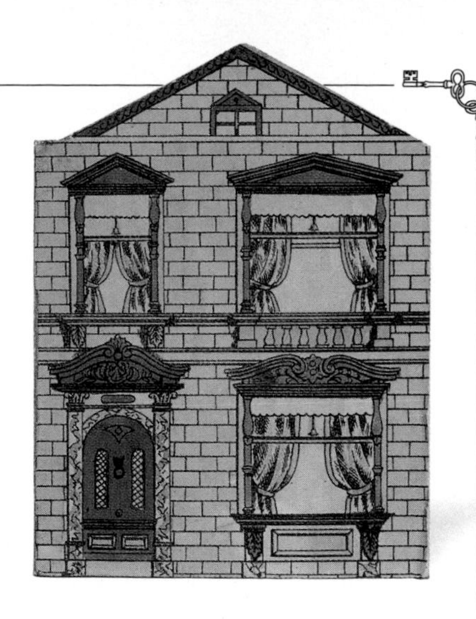

POLLOCK'S HOUSE *(ABOVE) This tiny one-up, one-down wooden dolls' house, with a hinged front, was made in the 1970s by John Gould who used one of Mr Pollock's nineteenth-century hand-coloured prints – depicting a brick wall with door and windows – as a facade.*

WOODEN DOLLS' HOUSE FURNITURE *(LEFT) These simple little pieces were selected to furnish a c.1917 Schoenhut bungalow. Metal fire-dogs hold the logs in a wooden fireplace with red brick-effect background; the small lamp is a modern, plastic replica.*

c.1900 LINEN CUPBOARD *(LEFT)*
Well stocked with household linen, bolts of cotton, sheets, and even mattress-stuffing, this decorative, painted wooden cupboard is a miniature version of the traditional linen cupboard that formed an important part of the dowries of southern German and Austrian brides.

LIGHT FIXTURE *(ABOVE)*
Known as a "gasolier", this gilded lead light fixture, with milk-glass globes, is from a c.*1880 French parlour. When electricity became popular, manufacturers adapted such fixtures by hanging them upside-down and using down-pointing bulbs and shades instead of globes.*

N, O

P, Q

R

S

T

U, V

AMERICAN DOLLS' HOUSE *(RIGHT) The earliest-known American dolls' house, this simple structure (dated 1744) has two rooms back and front with built-in fireplaces and painted windows on the sides.*

ACKNOWLEDGMENTS

AUTHOR'S ACKNOWLEDGMENTS

Many people have shared their knowledge and opened their dolls' houses to be photographed for this book. My most grateful thanks go particularly to Flora Gill Jacobs who, with her husband Ephraim, so graciously and helpfully made our time in their home and at the Washington Dolls' House & Toy Museum a very special episode.

Private collectors in England, too, unfailingly made their dolls' houses – and often their own homes – available to us; my special thanks go to Peggy and Dick Allen, Olivia Bristol, Moira Garland, Janet Gent, Michal Morse, and Suzie Vincent.

We were privileged also to be able to photograph dolls' houses in stately homes, museums, a shop, and an auction house; for their invaluable cooperation, my most appreciative thanks go to: Lord and Lady St Oswald and the staff at Nostell Priory; Roger Whitworth at the National Trust; John Guthrie and Claire Prout at Hever Castle; John Hodgson; Ann Jones and the staff at the Museum of Farnham; Dr Michael Eissenhauer, Dr Hermann Maué, and Dr Ulrike Heinrichs at the Germanisches Nationalmuseum, Nuremberg; Ella Hendricks and Helen Joustra at Frans Halsmuseum, Haarlem; Charlie Koens and Jurjen Creman at Centraal Museum, Haarlem; Juliet Wiggins at Playmobil (UK) Ltd; Mr and Mrs Pickering of the International Doll and Toy Collection; Michal Morse of The Dolls' House; and Olivia Bristol and Christine Jeffrey at Christie's, South Kensington.

My thanks go to everyone at Dorling Kindersley who helped with the book – an extra thank-you to Andrea Fair for deciphering my handwriting – with my warmest thanks to the Indomitable Trio, editor Irene Lyford, art editor Kevin Ryan, and photographer Matthew Ward, without whom the book could not have been produced and whose inspiration was only matched by their patience.

PUBLISHER'S ACKNOWLEDGMENTS

Dorling Kindersley would like to thank: Mr and Mrs Jacobs and the staff of the Washington Dolls' House & Toy Museum, Washington, D.C. for their very generous help and hospitality; Olivia Bristol for her unstinting help, expertise, and hospitality; staff at Nostell Priory, Wakefield; Germanisches Nationalmuseum, Nuremberg; Centraal Museum, Utrecht; and Frans Halsmuseum, Haarlem for invaluable access to collections, help, and advice; Andrea Fair for unfailing support, and for magically transforming handwritten copy into on-screen text; Charlotte Davies and Gillian Roberts for greatly appreciated editorial assistance; Michael Allaby for compiling the index; Julia Pashley for picture research; Murdo Culver for design assistance; and David Lyford for making the room set on page 11. In particular they would like to thank Matthew Ward and his assistant Rachel Leach for their unflagging patience and good humour in often difficult conditions.

COMMISSIONED ARTWORKS

We thank **Stephen Dew** for the house scale diagrams and other linework, and **Janos Marffy** for airbrush shadows.

PICTURE CREDITS

In the following acknowledgments, abbreviations with page numbers indicate position on page: t=top; b=bottom; c=centre; l=left; r=right

Bridgeman Art Library/Phillips 9tl; Christie's Fine Art Auctioneers 52bl, 132bl; Civico Museo Industriale Davia Bargelliri di Bologna 16b; Mary Evans Picture Library 6t, 132tr; Dave King Photo Library 143b; Peter Mattinson 132br; Nick Nicholson 7t, 7b, 14b, 15tl, 15tr, 15bl; Punch (1900) 140; The Royal Collection © Her Majesty Queen Elizabeth II 16t.

DOLLS' HOUSE COLLECTIONS/OWNERS/MANUFACTURERS

Centraal Museum, Utrecht 8, 24–5, 26–7, 28–9; Christies (South Kensington) Ltd 62–3, 82–3, 84–5, 135tl, 137bc, 139; Paul Cumbie 17; The Dolls' House, Covent Garden 133br; *The Dolls' House Carousel* © Bellew Publishing, Maggie Bateson & Herman Lelie, published in UK by Simon & Schuster 112tl; Dover Books: Sears, Roebuck & Co. Catalogs 75t, The New Pretty Village 87tl, 87tr, 87t; Faith Eaton Collection 3t, 4, 9tr, 11tr, 12bl, 12br, 13, 68–9, 76–7, 9, 72br, 73t, 94–5, 96–7, 98–9, 100–1, 102–3, 104–5, 110, 111b, 112tr, 112b, 113, 114–15, 116–17, 120–1, 122–3, 128–9, 130tr, 130br, 135tr, 137tc, 137tr, 137cl, 137br, 138, 141t, 142b; Museum of Farnham (long-term loan) 10t; Frans Halsmuseum, Haarlem 11tl, 34–5, 36–7, 136bl; Courtesy Moira Garland 54t, 119t; Janet Gent 137tl; Germanisches Nationalmuseum, Nuremberg 2, 18–19, 20–1, 22–3, 30–1, 32–3; Hever Castle Limited 11b, 48–9, 50–1, 133tl; Irene Lyford 130c; Mattel UK Ltd 113; Michal Morse Collection 11tr (contents); 72bl, 80–1; National Trust/St Oswald Collection: gatefold section; The Pickering Collection, Ethnic Doll & Toy Museum, England 53t, 124–5, 126–7; Playmobil (UK) Ltd 106–7, 108–9; Private Collections 1, 3b, 12t, 38–9, 40–1, 52br, 55b, 64–5, 74b, 131, 134br, 134tl, 136–7; Kevin Ryan 130bl; S.R. Vincent 53b, 75b, 86, 87bl, 87br, 111t, 141b; Washington Dolls' House & Toy Museum 5, 6b, 10b, 42–3, 44–5, 46–7, 54b, 55t, 56–7, 58–9, 60–1, 66–7, 70–1, 73b, 74t, 88–9, 90–1, 92–3, 118, 119b, 133tr, 135cr, 135br, 137cr, 137c, 142–3t, 144.

Every effort has been made to acknowledge owners and copyright-holders. Dorling Kindersley apologizes for any omissions.

HOUSE AND GARDEN
When the ingenious hinged garden folds up, its base forms the fourth wall of this decorative, twentieth-century German "red-roof" dolls' house with balconies, porch, and an ornamental gabled attic roof.